the FLORIDA
Bicycle Book

the FLORIDA Bicycle Book

Jackalene Crow Hiendlmayr

Pineapple Press, Inc.
Sarasota, Florida.

Inquiries should be addressed to Pineapple Press, Inc.,
P.O. Drawer 16008, Sarasota, FL 34239.

Library of Congress Cataloging-in-Publication Data

Hiendlmayr, Jackalene Crow, 1938–
    The Florida bicycle book / by Jackalene Crow Hien-
dlmayr. —1st ed.
        p.   cm.
    ISBN 0-910923-69-8 : $12.95
    1. Bicycle touring—Florida—Guide-books.
    2. Florida—Description and travel—1981-
—Guide-books.   I. Title.
GV1045.5.F6H54   1990
796.6'4'09759—dc20   89-48944
                                                           CIP

First edition

10 9 8 7 6 5 4 3 2 1

Design by Joan Lange Kresek
Typesetting by Hillsboro Printing, Tampa, Florida
Printed and bound by BookCrafters, Fredericksburg, Virginia

BE ADVISED: The fitness program described in this book, or
any such program derived from this program or otherwise, should
be conducted only upon medical clearance by a qualified physician.
The publisher and author disclaim liability for any claim brought
as the result of the use of this book or the program or tours herein
described.

To my husband, Frank, who felt there was a need for a book about the beauty of bicycling in Florida and had enough faith in me to know I could write it.

Contents

Acknowledgments

◆In writing this book, my husband and I solicited advice and suggestions from dozens of bicycle riders, some of whom have pedaled more miles than many people drive in their cars. Our thanks to all those cyclists. In particular, we wish to acknowledge the unending support of the following people:

Dan Burden, Tracy Suber, and Pat Pieratte of the Florida Department of Transportation who are responsible for creating a first-class bicycle program for Florida;

Greg Deal and Mary Ann Koos of the Division of Recreation and Planning at the Department of Natural Resources who are working on the formidable task of developing the Florida Rails-to-Trails program;

Myrna Haag, director of fitness training at the Tampa YMCA;

Dennis Scott of the Hillsborough County City-County Planning Commission who supplied us with information on bicycle clubs and organizations;

Bill Sparrowhawk, Hillsborough County Planning, and Renee Fauss, City of Tampa, both strong promoters of bicycle programs in Tampa;

Dr. Edgar Hirshberg, professor of English, University of South Florida, and patient proofreader;

John Bates, Sarasota cycling instructor, whose helpful suggestions improved the manuscript;

State Representatives Helen Gordon Davis and Patricia Bailey and Senators Jeanne Malchon, Betty Castor, Tom McPherson, and John Vogt, who were instrumental in passing the first Florida bicycle safety law, with special assistance from Senator Malcolm Beard;

Former Senator Pat Frank, aide Thalia Potter, and secretary Joan Hogarth, reliable sources of information about almost everything, including, but not limited to, bicycles;

Steve and Lea Yoczik of Fort Cooper State Park;

Ron Janus, who said we wouldn't write this book;

Dennis Tipton, who knew we would write this book;

Cycle Source of Pensacola, Rainbow Cycles of Tallahassee, Pedal Pushers of Jacksonville, Conway Bicycle Center of Orlando, The Bike Shop of Lake Wales, Bike Stop of Cape Coral, Snow's Cycle Shop of Naples, The Bicycle Center of Bradenton, Ringling Bicycle of Sarasota, Back to Basics of Lake Worth, and Dade Cycle Shop of Miami;

AND the whole gang at Dud Thames Bicycle Shop in Tampa, who patiently offered good advice throughout this project.

Introduction

◆ History tells us the first "real" bicycle was invented in 1839 in Scotland by a village blacksmith. It had iron tires and weighed 57 pounds and was the first vehicle on which a person could travel under his own power faster than he could run.

The bicycle has long been recognized as a sensible means of transportation, but in the United States automobiles replaced bicycles over the years as the preferred mode of travel. However, recent concerns about skyrocketing gasoline prices and air pollution, as well as the trend toward healthier living, have helped to bring about a rediscovery of the joys of bicycle riding, especially here in Florida. After all, a bicycle is still the most efficient means of movement man has ever devised.

At last count, almost half the residents of Florida, nearly six million of them, owned at least one bicycle. While some of these bicycles hang from hooks in garages gathering rust and spider webs, most bicycle owners ride at least once a week. There are also a few people whose bicycles are their only means of transportation. Many of these riders already know the joy of exploring our scenic state on a bicycle. This book will allow a lot more people to join them.

The Florida Bicycle Book is a complete reference and guide for people who want to tour Florida on a bicycle. The book is intended for anyone who can keep a two-wheeler upright, even if your longest bicycle trip until now has been to school or to the corner store. After reading this book you may be ready to become a bicycle tourist. Even if you aren't convinced that this should be your next great adventure, you will still find valuable information about Florida travel here. Just keep in mind that this book was written for day-trippers as much as for long-distance riders. And while you might start out as a weekend wanderer, you could end up planning the bicycle trip of a lifetime.

We are not recommending specific routes. You will need to buy a detailed road map of any area in which you plan to travel by bike. The maps provided here probably will not be detailed enough. You should carefully choose the route that you feel is suited to your own skills. What we have done is try to help you prepare for long-distance bicycle touring and provide you with information about where you can go and what you will find when you get there. We have included information on Florida Bicycle Trails designed by the state Department of Transportation (DOT) Bicycle Program and you can order detailed road maps of each bicycle trail as well as all the roads in every county from DOT after you have determined your route.

Part One will help you get you and your gear into shape for a safe and successful bicycle trip. "Florida Bicycling Facts" offers general information about Florida terrain and weather. Because safety is the primary concern of bicycle touring we also discuss specific information about the current state law governing bicycle riding in Florida. Also included are some special tips on safety while riding our roads. Remember that even when the law is on your side, you are greatly outweighed by someone in a car or truck and you must be constantly vigilant. Part One also covers first aid, conditioning, and diet, as well as clothing and equipment. If you're coming in from out of state and bringing your own bicycle, we offer several ways of transporting your bike to Florida. We also tell you where you can rent or buy a bicycle when you get here. We wrap up Part One with general information about motels, inns, and camping.

Part Two offers you a bicyclist's view of Florida. We provide information about state bicycle paths, bicycle clubs, bicycle events, and state parks where you can stop for a leisurely lunch, spend the night, or stay the whole weekend. To help you plan your trip, we have used the zoned planning map prepared by the state Department of Natural Resources (DNR), dividing the state into eleven regions and covering each region as thoroughly as possible.

Names and phone numbers of the people to contact at local bicycle clubs for further information and reservations are listed for each region. The Appendix includes a list of places to write for more detailed information. We found that one of the most valuable free publications available is the brochure titled, "Florida State Parks, The Real Florida," provided by DNR. This brochure includes a locator map of all the state parks and lists phone numbers to call at each park to make your reservations. DNR will also send you detailed brochures about any park or state attraction you want to visit.

We've tried to answer all the questions we had when we wanted information about bicycle journeys. We also asked many other riders what they would like to know about traveling in Florida on a bicycle. We hope that we have gathered here everything you need to know. Above all, we hope that you will get on your bike and discover the beauty, variety, and surprises our state has to offer.

Part One
Get Ready

Photograph by Pat Perdue

Chapter 1
Florida Bicycling Facts

In an effort to improve the use of outdoor facilities and assist in future planning, the Florida Department of Natural Resources (DNR) conducted a survey of visitors and residents throughout the state in 1987 to determine their favorite outdoor activities. The respondents were asked to rank various outdoor activities in order of enjoyment. To the surprise of the planners, but not to Florida bicyclists, the results of the survey indicate that bicycle riding is the third most popular outdoor activity in the state, surpassed only by saltwater beach activities and outdoor swimming pool use.

Terrain

The popularity of bicycle riding in Florida is certainly due in part to our relatively flat terrain. The state has no mountains and very few steep hills. The highest elevation point in Florida is 345 feet above sea level in northeast Walton County just below the Alabama border off State Route 331 at Paxton.

Physiographic Regions of Florida

This terrain map outlines five physical regions in Florida.

The **Western Highlands** are southward sloping, with hills and a few steep stream valleys.

The **Marianna Lowlands Region** has low rolling hills, numerous small lakes, and some interesting geological phenomena known as sinkholes. Sinkholes are created during long dry spells when the sand settles down around limestone deposits. Some of them are spectacularly deep. They have been known to swallow entire houses.

The **Tallahassee Hills Region** has long gentle slopes with rounded summits.

Extending from the Tallahassee Hills region to the Okefenokee Swamp in the north and almost to Lake Okeechobee in the south is the **Central Highlands Region**. The northern part is mostly level plains, and the western part is a mix of hills and broad low plains. To the east and south in this region is the Lake subregion with numerous lakes and hills up to 325 feet above sea level.

The **Coastal Lowlands Region** follows the coastline, including the Florida Keys and extending inward as much as 60 miles at some points.

Weather

Adding to the ease of pedaling our flat terrain is the state's delightful year-round weather. While people in Minnesota and Montana begin to put up their storm windows and get out their heavy winter clothing, outdoor lovers in Florida will find winter one of the best times of the year to get out and ride.

If you are a year-round resident you know you should plan to take a lengthy bicycle trip during the cooler months, from October through April. The summer heat is best for beach and pool activities. If you do ride in the summer, mornings are the best time. Severe afternoon showers are common during the summer months.

Florida is closer to the equator than is any other part of the continental United States. This means subtropical weather: lots of rain and high humidity during the hot summer months and winters that are fairly dry and cool with only occasional frosts in the northern regions. Nowhere in the state are you more than 70 miles from either the Atlantic or the Gulf coasts and sea breezes help moderate seasonal temperature extremes. In the winter months, Florida has more sunshine per day than any other eastern state. That's why we call it the Sunshine State!

Average Monthly Temperature and Precipitation—By Zone

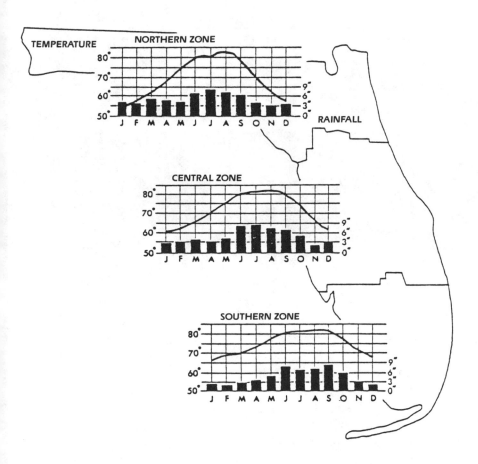

Florida Mean Temperatures — Maximum/Minimum
From the records of the National Weather Service

	JAN.	FEB.	MAR.	APR.	MAY	JUNE	JULY	AUG.	SEPT.	OCT.	NOV.	DEC.
Apalachicola	61 / 46	63 / 48	68 / 54	75 / 61	82 / 68	86 / 74	87 / 75	88 / 75	85 / 72	78 / 63	69 / 53	63 / 48
Daytona Beach	69 / 48	70 / 49	74 / 53	80 / 59	85 / 65	88 / 70	90 / 72	89 / 73	87 / 72	81 / 65	75 / 55	70 / 49
Fort Myers	75 / 52	76 / 53	80 / 57	85 / 62	89 / 66	90 / 72	91 / 74	91 / 74	90 / 73	85 / 67	80 / 59	76 / 54
Jacksonville	65 / 44	67 / 46	72 / 50	79 / 57	85 / 64	88 / 70	90 / 72	90 / 72	86 / 70	79 / 62	71 / 51	66 / 45
Key West	76 / 66	77 / 66	79 / 70	82 / 74	85 / 76	88 / 79	89 / 80	89 / 80	88 / 79	84 / 75	80 / 71	76 / 67
Lakeland	70 / 51	72 / 52	76 / 56	82 / 62	87 / 67	90 / 71	90 / 73	90 / 73	88 / 72	82 / 66	76 / 57	71 / 52
Miami	76 / 59	77 / 59	79 / 63	83 / 67	85 / 71	88 / 74	89 / 75	90 / 76	88 / 75	85 / 71	80 / 64	77 / 60
Orlando	70 / 50	72 / 51	76 / 56	81 / 61	87 / 66	89 / 71	90 / 73	90 / 73	88 / 72	82 / 66	76 / 57	71 / 51
Pensacola	61 / 43	64 / 45	69 / 51	77 / 59	84 / 66	89 / 72	90 / 74	90 / 74	86 / 70	80 / 60	70 / 49	63 / 44
Tallahassee	64 / 41	66 / 43	72 / 48	80 / 56	87 / 63	90 / 70	91 / 72	90 / 72	87 / 69	81 / 58	71 / 46	65 / 41
Tampa	71 / 50	72 / 52	76 / 56	82 / 62	87 / 67	90 / 72	90 / 74	90 / 74	89 / 73	84 / 65	77 / 56	72 / 51
West Palm Beach . . .	75 / 56	76 / 56	79 / 60	83 / 65	86 / 69	88 / 72	90 / 74	90 / 74	88 / 75	84 / 70	79 / 62	76 / 57

The warm sunny days and cool nights make Florida an outdoor paradise, but there are also hazards. Violent thunderstorms and the danger of lightning are a daily risk in the summer. There are more people hit by lightning in Florida than in any other state. Lightning is particularly dangerous near water. Take the following precautions to reduce your chances of being hit:

Watch for towering thunderheads and flashes of lightning in the distance as a signal to take cover.

Take along a portable battery-powered radio and pay attention to weather forecasts.

If you are caught out in the open, seek out a low-lying area but stay away from large trees.

Get out of and away from open water.

Stay away from wire fences or metal signposts.

If you feel your hair stand on end, this is an indication that lightning may be about to strike. Drop to your knees but do not lie flat on the ground.

If you are riding with a group and are caught in a storm, spread out so that if lightning strikes it won't catch everyone.

Bicycle Safety Laws

Below you will find portions of the Florida Statutes that apply to bicycles. Read them over so that you know and understand the laws as they are written. Remember that the best way to avoid accidents is to follow the traffic laws and stay alert. As you read the laws, keep in mind that they apply to automobile drivers as well as bicyclists. Except for certain special regulations, the same laws govern both riding a bicycle and driving a car, but because bicycles are lighter and less powerful than cars, bicyclists must be especially cautious on the road.

State Uniform Traffic Control — Ch. 316 as of 1988

316.003 Definitions. — *The following words and phrases, when used in this chapter, shall have the mean-*

Photograph by Pat Perdue

ings respectively ascribed to them in this section, except where the context otherwise requires:

(2) Bicycle.   Every vehicle propelled solely by human power, and every motorized bicycle propelled by a combination of human power and an electric helper motor rated at not more than 200 watts and capable of propelling the vehicle at a speed of not more than 10 miles per

hour on level ground upon which any person may ride, having two tandem wheels, and including any device generally recognized as a bicycle though equipped with two front or two rear wheels. The term does not include such a vehicle with a seat height of no more than 25 inches from the ground when the seat is adjusted to its highest level position or a scooter or similar device.

(63) Bicycle Path. *Any road, path, or way that is open to bicycle travel, which road, path, or way is physically separated from motorized vehicular traffic by an open space or by a barrier and is located either within the highway right-of-way or within an independent right-of-way.*

316.091 Limited access facilities; interstate highways; use restricted.

(2) Except as provided herein, no person shall operate upon a limited access facility any bicycle, motor-driven cycle, animal-drawn vehicle, or any other vehicle which by its design or condition is incompatible with the safe and expedient movement of traffic.

(4) No person shall operate a bicycle on the roadway or along the shoulder of an interstate highway.

316.2065 Bicycle Regulations

(1) Every person propelling a vehicle by human power has all of the rights and all of the duties applicable to the driver of any other vehicle under this chapter, except as to special regulations in this chapter, and except as to provisions of this chapter which by their nature can have no application.

(2) A person operating a bicycle may not ride other than upon or astride a permanent and regular seat attached thereto.

(3) No bicycle may be used to carry more persons at one time than the number which it is designed or equipped, except that an adult rider may carry a child securely attached to his person in a backpack or sling.

(4) No person riding upon any bicycle, coaster, roller skates, sled, or toy vehicle may attach the same or himself to any vehicle upon a roadway. This subsection may not prohibit attaching a bicycle trailer or bicycle semi-trailer to a bicycle if that trailer or semitrailer has been designed for such attachment and solely for carrying cargo.

(5)(a) Any person operating a bicycle upon a roadway at less than the normal speed of traffic at the time and place and under the conditions then existing shall ride as close as practicable to the right-hand curb or edge of the roadway except under any of the following situations:

1. When overtaking and passing another bicycle or vehicle proceeding in the same direction.

2. When preparing for a left turn at an intersection or into a private road or driveway.

3. When reasonably necessary to avoid any condition, including, but not limited to, a fixed or moving object, parked or moving vehicle, bicycle, pedestrian, animal, surface hazard, or substandard width lane, that makes it unsafe to continue along the right-hand curb or edge. For the purposes of this subsection, a "substandard width lane" is a lane that is too narrow for a bicycle and another vehicle to travel safely side by side within the lane.

(b) Any person operating a bicycle upon a one-way highway with two or more marked traffic lanes may ride as near the left-hand curb or edge of such roadway as practicable.

(c) Persons riding bicycles upon a roadway may not ride more than two abreast except on paths or parts of roadways set aside for the exclusive use of bicycles. Persons riding two abreast may not impede traffic when traveling at less than the normal speed of traffic at the time and place and under the conditions then existing and shall ride within a single lane.

(7) Any person operating a bicycle shall keep at least one hand upon the handlebars.

(8) Every bicycle in use between sunset and sunrise shall be equipped with a lamp on the front exhibiting a white light visible from a distance of at least 500 feet to the front and a lamp and reflector on the rear each exhibiting a red light visible from a distance of 600 feet to the rear. A bicycle or its rider may be equipped with lights or reflectors in addition to those required by this section.

(9) No parent of any minor child and no guardian of any minor ward may authorize or knowingly permit any such minor child or ward to violate any of the provisions of this section.

(10) A person propelling a vehicle by human power upon and along a sidewalk, or across a roadway upon and along a crosswalk, has all of the rights and duties applicable to a pedestrian under the same circumstances.

(11) A person propelling a bicycle upon and along a sidewalk, or across a roadway upon and along a crosswalk, shall yield the right-of-way to any pedestrian and shall give an audible signal before overtaking and passing such pedestrian.

(12) No person upon roller skates, or riding in or by means of any coaster, toy vehicle, or similar device, may go upon any roadway except while crossing a street on a crosswalk; and, when so crossing, such person shall be granted all rights and shall be subject to all of the duties applicable to pedestrians.

(13) This section shall not apply upon any street while set aside as a play street authorized herein or as designated by state, county, or municipal authority.

(14) Every bicycle shall be equipped with a brake or brakes which will enable its rider to stop the bicycle within 25 feet from a speed of 10 miles per hour on dry, level, clean pavement.

(15) A person engaged in the business of selling bicycles at retail shall not sell any bicycle unless the bicycle has an identifying number permanently stamped or cast on its frame.

316.151 Required position and method of turning at intersections.

(1) The driver of a vehicle intending to turn at an intersection shall do so as follows:

(a) Right turn.   *Both the approach for a right turn and a right turn shall be made as close as practicable to the right-hand curb or edge of the roadway.*

(b) Left turn.   *The driver of a vehicle intending to turn left at any intersection shall approach the intersec-*

tion in the extreme left-hand lane lawfully available to
traffic moving in the direction of such vehicle, and, after
entering the intersection, the left turn shall be made so
as to leave the intersection in a lane lawfully available
to traffic moving in such direction upon the roadway
being entered. A person riding a bicycle and intending
to turn left in accordance with this section is entitled to
the full use of the lane from which the turn may legally
be made. Whenever practicable the left turn shall be
made in that portion of the intersection to the left of the
center of the intersection.

(c) Left turn by bicycle.   In addition to the method of
making a left turn described in paragraph (b), a person
riding a bicycle and intending to turn left has the option
of following the course described hereafter: The rider
shall approach the turn as close as practicable to the
right curb or edge of the roadway; after proceeding
across the intersecting roadway, the turn shall be made
as close as practicable to the curb or edge of the roadway
on the far side of the intersection; and, before proceeding, the bicyclist shall comply with any official traffic
control device or police officer regulating traffic along
the highway along which he intends to proceed.

(2) The state, county, and local authorities in their
respective jurisdictions may cause official traffic control
devices to be placed within or adjacent to intersections
and thereby require that a different course from that
specified in this section be traveled by vehicles turning
at an intersection. When such devices are so placed, no
driver of a vehicle may turn a vehicle at an intersection
other than as directed and required by such devices.

316.155 When signal required.

(1) No person may turn a vehicle from a direct course upon a highway unless and until such movement can be made with reasonable safety, and then only after giving an appropriate signal in the manner hereinafter provided, in the event any other vehicle may be affected by the movement.

(2) A signal of intention to turn right or left must be given continuously during not less than the last 100 feet traveled by the vehicle before turning, except that such a signal by hand or arm need not be given continuously by a bicyclist if the hand is needed in the control or operation of the bicycle.

(3) No person may stop or suddenly decrease the speed of a vehicle without first giving an appropriate signal in the manner provided herein to the driver of any vehicle immediately to the rear, when there is opportunity to give such signal.

(4) The signals provided for in s. 316.156 shall be used to indicate an intention to turn and may not, except as provided in s. 316.2397, be flashed as a courtesy or "do pass" signal to operators of other vehicles approaching from the rear.

316.157 Method of giving hand and arm signals.

All signals herein required to be given by hand and arm shall be given from the left side of the vehicle in the following manner and such signals shall indicate as follows:

(1) Left turn.   *Hand and arm extended horizontally.*

(2) Right turn. *Hand and arm extended upward, except that a bicyclist may extend the right hand and arm horizontally to the right side of the bicycle.*

(3) Stop or decrease speed. *Hand and arm extended downward.*

316.1575 Obedience to traffic control devices at railroad-highway grade crossings.

(1) Any person walking or driving a vehicle and approaching a railroad-highway grade crossing under any of the circumstances stated in this section shall stop within 50 feet but not less than 15 feet from the nearest rail of such railroad and shall not proceed until he can do so safely. The foregoing requirements apply when:

(a) A clearly visible electric or mechanical signal device gives warning of the immediate approach of a railroad train;

(b) A crossing gate is lowered or a human flagman gives or continues to give a signal of the approach or passage of a railroad train;

(c) An approaching railroad train emits an audible signal or the railroad train, by reason of its speed or nearness to the crossing, is an immediate hazard; or

(d) An approaching railroad train is plainly visible and is in hazardous proximity to the railroad-highway grade crossing, regardless of the type of traffic control devices installed at the crossing.

(2) No person shall drive any vehicle through, around, or under any crossing gate while the gate or barrier is being opened or closed.

316.172 Traffic to stop for school bus.

(1) Any person using, operating, or driving a vehicle on or over the roads or highways of this state shall, upon approaching any school bus used in transporting school pupils to or from school which is properly identified in substantial accordance with the provisions of s. 234.051 and which displays a stop signal, bring such vehicle to a full stop while the bus is stopped, and the vehicle shall not pass the school bus until the signal has been withdrawn. Pursuant to the provisions of s. 318.18(7), any person who violates the provisions of this subsection shall be subject to a penalty of $100. In addition to such penalty, for a second or subsequent offense within a period of 4 years, the department shall suspend the driver's license of the person for a period of not less than 90 days nor more than 6 months.

(2) The driver of a vehicle upon a divided highway where the one-way roadways are separated by an intervening unpaved space of at least 5 feet or physical barrier need not stop upon meeting or passing a school bus which is on a different roadway.

(3) Every school bus shall stop as far to the right of the street as possible before discharging or loading passengers and, when possible, shall not stop where the visibility is obscured for a distance of 200 feet either way from the bus.

316.1945 Stopping, standing, or parking prohibited in specified places.

(1) Except when necessary to avoid conflict with other traffic, or in compliance with law or the directions of a police officer or official traffic control device, no person shall:

(a) Stop, stand, or park a vehicle:
1. On the roadway side of any vehicle stopped or parked at the edge or curb of a street.
2. On a sidewalk.
3. Within an intersection.
4. On a crosswalk.
5. Between a safety zone and the adjacent curb or within 30 feet of points on the curb immediately opposite the ends of a safety zone, unless the Department of Transportation indicates a different length by signs or markings.
6. Alongside or opposite any street excavation or obstruction when stopping, standing, or parking would obstruct traffic.
7. Upon any bridge or other elevated structure upon a highway or within a highway tunnel.
8. On any railroad tracks.
9. On a bicycle path.
10. At any place where official traffic control devices prohibit stopping.
11. On the roadway or shoulder of a limited access facility, except as provided by regulation of the Department of Transportation, or on the paved portion of a connecting ramp; except that a vehicle which is disabled or in a condition improper to be driven as a result of mechanical failure or accident may be parked on such shoulder for a period not to exceed 6 hours. This provision is not applicable to a person stopping a vehicle to render aid to an injured person or assistance to a disabled vehicle in obedience to the directions of a law enforcement officer or to a person stopping a vehicle in compliance with applicable traffic laws.

12. For the purpose of loading or unloading a passenger on the paved roadway or shoulder of a limited access facility or on the paved portion of any connecting ramp. This provision is not applicable to a person stopping a vehicle to render aid to an injured person or assistance to a disabled vehicle.

(b) Stand or park a vehicle, whether occupied or not, except momentarily to pick up or discharge a passenger or passengers:

1. In front of a public or private driveway.

2. Within 15 feet of a fire hydrant.

3. Within 20 feet of a crosswalk at an intersection.

4. Within 30 feet upon the approach to any flashing signal, stop sign, or traffic control signal located at the side of a roadway.

5. Within 20 feet of the driveway entrance to any fire station and on the side of a street opposite the entrance to any fire station within 75 feet of such entrance (when properly signposted).

6. On an exclusive bicycle lane.

7. An any place where official traffic control devices prohibit standing.

(c) Park a vehicle, whether occupied or not, except temporarily for the purpose of, and while actually engaged in, loading or unloading merchandise or passengers:

1. Within 50 feet of the nearest rail of a railroad crossing unless the Department of Transportation establishes a different distance due to unusual circumstances.

2. At any place where official signs prohibit parking.

(2) No person shall move a vehicle not lawfully under his control to any such prohibited area or away from a curb such a distance as is unlawful.

(3) A law enforcement officer or parking enforcement specialist who discovers a vehicle parked in violation of this section or a municipal or county ordinance may:

(a) Issue a ticket form as may be used by a political subdivision or municipality to the driver; or

(b) If the vehicle is unattended, attach such ticket to the vehicle in a conspicuous place, except that the uniform traffic citation prepared by the department pursuant to s. 316.650 may not be issued by being attached to an unattended vehicle.

The uniform traffic citation prepared by the department pursuant to s. 316.650 may not be issued for violation of a municipal or county parking ordinance.

316.1995 Driving upon sidewalk or bicycle path.

No person shall drive any vehicle other than by human power upon a bicycle path, sidewalk, or sidewalk area, except upon a permanent or duly authorized temporary driveway.

Safety Tips

When riding with traffic, keep in mind that drivers don't want an accident any more than you do, but as the bicyclist, you are at a disadvantage, so always use caution. Besides obeying the law, we also suggest that you follow these general rules of bicycle safety.

1. Stay on your side of the road, traveling with traffic and as near to the curb as road conditions permit.

Photograph by Dan Burden

2. Remain steady when a vehicle is approaching you from behind and allow them to pass you safely.

3. Always signal with your hand if you are going to turn or merge with traffic. You can also wave with your hand to have someone pass you or hold up your hand if you are going to stop.

4. Look back at approaching motorists to let them know you are aware of them and are trying to allow them safe passage.

5. Watch at intersections ahead for cars pulling out. Keep an eye out at all times for cars making right or left turns. Always remember than you can stop much faster than a car, and your own alertness is your best protection.

6. If you are riding at night, wear reflecting strips on your clothing, and be sure you have plenty of lights and reflectors on your bike.

7. Practice riding on quiet streets first.

8. Ride single file in traffic.

9. Ride the right way on one-way streets.

10. Don't run red lights.

11. Don't wear radio headsets that block your ability to hear traffic.

12. Wear a protective helmet at all times.

Try to pick a route that you can enjoy, not one where you are fighting for your life. Follow the traffic laws as if you were driving an automobile. We would like to point out that only one out of five bicycle accidents involves an automobile. Most bicycle accidents occur when the rider hits a pothole, loose gravel, or other road hazards.

There is a training program available to assist you with bicycle safety skills. For information, contact the League of American Wheelmen in Florida and ask about the "Effective Cycling" program. John Bates is the man to speak with (see Appendix).

Roadways Closed to Bicycles

The following is a list of Florida roadways closed to travel by bicycle provided by the state Department of Transportation (DOT). Every effort was made to compile a complete list. However, if you find others, please let DOT know.

All interstate highways, limited (controlled) access highways, and expressways are closed to bicycle travel.

Jacksonville: Roosevelt Boulevard connector (part of U.S. 17, State Road 15); J. Turner Butler Boulevard (State Road 202).

Merritt Island: Bennett Causeway (State Road 528 becoming State Road A1A).

Satellite Beach: Pineda Causeway (County Road 404).

Fort Myers: Sanibel Causeway (County Road 867); Caloosahatchee Bridge (U.S. 41). Note that Edison Bridge (Business U.S. 41) *is* open to bicycles.

Miami: Julia Tuttle Causeway (U.S. I-95); MacArthur Causeway (U.S. 41/State Road A1A).

Chapter 2
Physical Fitness

First Aid

First aid is of vital importance to the bicycle rider. When you ride a bicycle every day, or ride long distances, you need to be prepared both for occasional mishaps and more serious emergencies. You might fall and scrape a knee or an elbow, but the possibility of an accident is even greater on long rides when you are under strain. You must be tuned in to the needs and condition of your body and learn to recognize danger signals. You can become overheated, start to develop blisters, or put too much strain on your muscles. You must heed the warning signals and know how to treat them.

The first-aid kit should be well stocked—this is not the place to skimp! The kit should include Band-Aids, aspirin, a good rub-in salve for sore muscles, an antiseptic cream for occasional scrapes or bug bites, and, especially

if you're camping, a snake-bite kit. A supply of good
sunscreen lotion (at least no. 15) and some effective bug
spray for the night stops should be included in your pack.

If you've lived in Florida for a few years, you're probably already accustomed to our weather conditions. If
you're coming in from out of state or out of the country,
it's better to plan your bicycle trip during the cooler
months of the year from October through April. One of
the most common health problems caused by our
weather is sunburn. Sunburn can be very painful, and
even in the winter or on cloudy days exposed skin should
be protected with a sunscreen lotion. Heat cramps, heat
exhaustion, and heat stroke can occur if you are not
accustomed to outdoor activities. Heat cramps or heat
exhaustion can usually be treated by resting in a cool
place and sipping water. In cases where heat stroke is
suspected, the victim should be taken to a doctor immediately. Hypothermia can also occur if a rider gets wet
and is exposed to lower temperatures and wind. If you
begin to feel chilled and start shivering, stop and seek
warm shelter. If you are camping, put up your tent and
get into dry clothes and your sleeping bag.

Heat cramps are caused by loss of body chemicals, and
drinking plain water will not take care of this problem. A
number of high-energy drinks are available that have
been designed to replace body chemicals lost during
stressful exercise. Heat stroke can be very dangerous;
symptoms include nausea, dizziness, skin that is hot and
flushed, and rapid breathing. This condition calls for
immediate treatment by a doctor.

If you are caught out in a storm and a rider is struck
by lightning, you should be prepared to administer

mouth-to-mouth resuscitation. If there is no pulse, someone who is trained should administer CPR.

It's been said that the mosquito should be named the state bird of Florida. Mosquitos grow to a healthy size and are year-round pests in the state, whatever the weather. They won't bother you while you're riding, but they can make camping miserable. If you're bitten excessively, you could become ill. It's easy to handle this problem by carrying along a good insect repellent that you know is effective for you. Avoid wearing fragrances such as perfume or after-shave lotion.

Another biting insect in Florida is the fire ant. Whenever you stop to take a break, watch out for anthills (large or small mounds of sand with a hole in the center). If you set up your tent on top of an anthill, you'll have company before morning, and fire ants do sting painfully. Some people are allergic to their sting and can have very severe reactions. If you are allergic to any kind of insect sting or bite, be sure to ask your doctor about what to bring with you on a long bike ride.

Many people fear snakes far more than insect bites. You should learn which snakes in Florida are poisonous and how to avoid their likely habitats. If you keep your eyes open and let them have their own space, you shouldn't have any trouble. Include a snake-bite kit in your first-aid kit and know how to use it.

The best way to be ready for a medical emergency is to take a Red Cross course in first aid before you leave home. Don't panic if an accident occurs. Just be prepared!

Photograph by Pat Perdue

Fitness Training

An occasional ride to the store or to school or even a day-long ride with friends is very different from setting out on a weekend trip or a two-week vacation on your bicycle. A lot of preparation and training are needed before you begin a long bicycle trip. If you are loafing along looking at the scenery and carrying heavy packs, you may travel only 25 to 30 miles per day. But stop and think for a moment: pedaling a bicycle 25 to 30 miles per day adds up to as much as 210 miles in a week. A trip like this requires a rider who is in good physical condition. You don't want to set out on a scenic vacation and then spend three or four days of that vacation staring at the walls of a motel or the inside of a tent waiting for a pulled muscle to ease. Your pretrip planning should begin with a thorough conditioning program to help you avoid that problem.

The fitness advice and conditioning chart included in this section were prepared by Myrna Haag, fitness director of the Tampa YMCA. She is certified by the YMCA in fitness education and has taken courses at the American College of Sports Medicine in exercise fitness, kinesiology, nutrition, and cardiac rehabilitation. She also competed in the 1988 Hawaiian Iron Man triathlon. The conditioning chart she has prepared is a four-month plan for becoming fit enough to pedal 250–300 miles in one week.

"Whatever the shape you're in," says Myrna, "you should begin your conditioning program at least four months before you plan to take your long ride. If you haven't had a physical checkup recently, get one now. Always begin with stretching and limbering exercises before and after exercises or a ride. Don't try to stretch too much at first—you'll tear your muscles. Just stretch enough to feel it. Stretching improves your flexibility and relieves stiffness and soreness. And remember, stretching means a slow steady reach, not bouncing and jerking."

Conditioning Chart

W = Weight Work for 30 minutes
B = Bicycle Riding

Week	Monday	Tuesday	Wednesday	Thursday	Friday	Saturday
1	W B–20 min.	B–25 min.	W B–20 min.	Rest	W B–20 min.	B–30 min.
2	W B–20 min.	B–30 min.	W B–20 min.	Rest	W B–20 min.	B–35 min.
3	W B–20 min.	B–35 min.	W B–20 min.	Rest	W B–20 min.	B–40 min.
4*	W B–25 min.	B–35 min.	W B–25 min.	Rest	W B–25 min.	B–45 min.
5	W B–25 min.	B–35 min.	W B–25 min.	Rest	W B–25 min.	B–45 min.
6	W B–30 min.	B–40 min.	W B–30 min.	Rest	W B–30 min.	B–50 min.
7	W B–30 min.	B–45 min.	W B–30 min.	Rest	W B–30 min.	B–60 min.
8	W B–35 min.	B–50 min.	W B–35 min.	Rest	W B–35 min.	B–70 min.
9	W B–45 min.	B–60 min.	W B–35 min.	Rest	W B–35 min.	B–80 min.
10	W B–45 min.	B–70 min.	W B–40 min.	Rest	W B–40 min.	B–90 min.
11	W B–50 min.	B–80 min.	W B–45 min.	Rest	W B–45 min.	B–110 min.
12	W B–60 min.	B–90 min.	W B–45 min.	Rest	W B–50 min.	B–120 min.
13	W B–60 min.	B–90 min.	W B–45 min.	Rest	W B–50 min.	B–120 min.

Conditioning Chart

W = Weight Work for 30 minutes
B = Bicycle Riding

Week	Monday	Tuesday	Wednesday	Thursday	Friday	Saturday
14	W B–100 min.	B–110 min.	W B–60 min.	Rest	W B–60 min.	B–120 min.
15	W B–105 min.	B–110 min.	W B–60 min.	Rest	W B–70 min.	B–135 min.
16	W B–105 min.	B–110 min.	W B–60 min.	W B–60 min.	Rest	Rest

*Week 4 routine can be extended an additional four weeks by those who need to build a stronger base (e.g., beginning, overweight, or out-of-shape cyclists).

When you begin your conditioning program you are building a "base." The stronger your base, the less likely you are to have muscle injuries or to suffer from fatigue. To develop a strong base it is best to pedal more miles over a longer span of time. In other words, it is better to cycle the times on the chart for four to six months prior to your trip than to try to cycle twice as far for only two to three months. You need time for your muscles to grow and rest. Rushing your miles could lead to exercise overload and result in an injury. Note too that if you are a beginner rider or very overweight, you should extend your training from week 4 on the chart for at least six weeks, rather than just two, before going on with the program. This helps you build a stronger base.

It is very important that you have a total body conditioning program to prepare for long-distance cycling. You will use more than just your legs and heart. Your entire upper body will become fatigued from riding long hours.

Three times a week you should do strength work on
shoulders, arms, back, neck, stomach, and chest. This is
best accomplished using weight equipment. Sit-ups and
push-ups can compensate if weight-lifting machines are
not available. If you go to a gym to use machines, be
sure there are people who can instruct you in the proper
use of the machines. Your local YMCA or YWCA will
likely have the machines and assistance you need.

Walking is another good way to begin to get in shape.
Many public parks have walking paths with an area
where you can stop and do some limbering exercises. You
can judge for yourself how much conditioning you need as
you increase your riding distances during the pretrip
planning stage. Some cyclists recommend that you work
out first on a stationary bicycle until you build up your
legs a little. Riding on a real bike means that you
actually have less training time because of cruising and
stop signs, while stationary bikes give you continuous
riding. The times on the chart are for riding a real bike,
and if you have a stationary bike you can decrease your
training time by at least 25 percent.

Duration, frequency, and intensity are critical in
developing fitness. Duration means at least one long bike
ride per week. This helps the body get used to long distances. After a long endurance ride, it is recommended
that the rider take the next day off to allow the body to
recover. You should not ride the full distance until you
actually take your trip.

Frequency means it is best to ride five times per week
with two days off to recover. Less than five times per
week is not enough frequency, and more than five times

per week may not allow your body to recover from prior workouts.

Intensity is a factor after you have built a strong base. The shorter rides can have a higher intensity; the longer rides should be much lighter in intensity. You should concentrate more on the distance during the long ride.

When you stop for a break, don't sit down right away because your muscles will cramp. Walk around a little and do your stretching exercises. Once you're out on the road, you'll find that you need those exercises to get started in the morning.

Diet

As you increase your activity, your diet should include an increased amount of carbohydrates, such as bananas, pears, breads, cereals, and pastas. Try to eliminate high-saturated animal fat foods like fried chicken and hamburgers, as well as French fries, onion rings, and potato chips. You should also avoid refined sugars and junk foods.

When you're on the road you may be tempted to stop at a hamburger stand instead of buying a nutritious meal at a restaurant or cooking one at your campfire. At those times, you must remember you are not just filling an empty space, but taking on the fuel that will enable you to complete your trip.

Carry a water bottle on your bike and take occasional sips as you ride. Some riders carry juices in their bottles, but juice just doesn't quench your thirst as well and can leave a bittersweet taste in your mouth. Plain water refreshes with no aftertaste. On your long trip you can

Photograph by Pat Perdue

look forward to drinking juice when you stop for lunch or
for the day. Eat small meals during the day when you
are pedaling and snack between meals on bananas and
other high-protein foods. And remember, when it's all
over, your body will need time to get back in the every-

day groove. When you return to your regular routine, you'll miss the long periods of exercise. Be prepared for some letdown unless you keep up your conditioning program.

Chapter 3
Equipment

Bicycles

At this point you've probably decided that your old single-speed with coaster brakes is not going to hold up too well over the long haul. Don't run out and take a second mortgage on your house to buy the dream bicycle. A sturdy, dependable touring bicycle can be found for less than $300. Take the time to learn what you need to make your ride as comfortable as possible, then shop around.

Make sure the bicycle you select has a frame size that fits your body size and proportions. The frame should be strong but not too heavy. A lighter bike is easier to pedal and, depending on the alloy used in the frame, may also be tougher. The choice of gearing, whether it's a three- or five- or ten-speed, is up to you. You need a high gear for flat terrain and a low gear for climbing hills, with medium and high gears for cruising downhill.

While we're talking about cruising down hills, be sure
you check out the brakes. They should be thoroughly
tested and adjusted. It's tough to suffer through a long
hill climb in the wrong gear, but it's even tougher to cat-
apult down the other side of the hill with bad brakes.
And don't forget to spend a lot of time selecting the right
saddle. While the wide, springy seat might look good,
you'll soon learn the narrow, firm leather seat will not
rub as great an area of your body on the long rides.

There are as many choices in tires as there are in bicycles, and the decision on what tires you'll need depends
on the type of surface on which you plan to do most of
your traveling. You can use the thin high-pressure tires
for smooth road travel, but for gravel or sandy roads and
beaches, a wider, low-pressure tire is your best bet. Just
be sure to carry extra tubes for your tires and invest in
a tire pump that attaches to the frame of your bike.
Carry a patch kit and know how to use it.

When you get really serious about taking a long bicycle
trip, your best bet is to find a dependable bicycle dealer,
one whose shop is devoted to bicycle sales and service.
Let the salespeople guide you in your outfitting needs.
They can help you select the right equipment and adjust
it to fit your needs. The proper selection and fitting of
your bicycle can mean the difference between the trip of
your dreams and a vacation nightmare. If the bicycle is
not adjusted to your height and reach, you will soon be
in serious pain. It doesn't cost any more to have a dealer
help you with these adjustments. He wants you to have a
good riding experience.

Ask your dealer to show you how to do basic bicycle
repairs on the road. For instance, you might have to

Photograph by Pat Perdue

replace a spoke and true the wheel, at least well enough
to get you to a shop. Carry a small tool kit for minor
problems and be sure you know what to do with it. A
good dealer will stand behind the equipment he sells you.
Even if you're a long way from home and you have problems, you can usually find another dealer who carries
your brand and can help you.

Clothing

"Dress for success" applies to bicyle touring in a big
way. In Florida, bicycle touring usually requires lightweight clothing that protects you from the sun any time
of the year. Depending on the season and on the section
of the state you plan to tour, you may also need some
long pants and a hooded sweatshirt to wear in the evening. Several T-shirts with long sleeves and a few pairs
of shorts should be sufficient for riding. Socks should
always be worn to absorb sweat and protect your feet.
It's a good idea to hand-wash your clothes at the end
of each day, rinsing them thoroughly. Wearing sweaty
clothes day after day can cause a rash or blisters. Get
some rain gear that's designed to let your skin breathe.

A helmet might be a little uncomfortable when you
first begin to wear one, but you will get used to it and it
might even save your life. Start wearing one every time
you ride, and by the time you're ready to begin your
trip, you'll feel naked without one.

If you want to avoid blisters on your hands, you should
also buy bicycling gloves when you begin your training.
They have padded leather palms and no fingers. They
provide some comfort to your hands during long periods
of holding onto the handlebars. If you ever take a spill
and put your hands out to break your fall, the gloves will
protect you.

The special clothing designed for competitive riders
can be very useful for the touring rider as well. This
clothing is optional but highly recommended. It includes
the short pants with a fleece or chamois lining in the seat
area. Actually, the lined shorts could be as important as

the gloves and helmet on a long ride. Shoes designed to fit on the pedals can be very helpful as well.

Shipping Your Bicycle

We conducted a survey of airlines, bus companies, and Amtrak to provide this information about bicycle shipping for those of you coming to Florida from out of state or out of the country.

Photograph courtesy of Dan Burden.

Almost all of the airlines surveyed prefer that you remove your handlebars and pedals and place your bike in a bag or box. If you care enough about your bicycle to bring it with you, then care enough to package it in such a way that it will arrive safely. It would be tragic to pay the cost of shipping and then find the bicycle is damaged so badly that you can't ride it.

Some airlines will provide the bag or box, while others require that you provide the package. For example, American Airlines charges $10 for a bag and $15 for a box. They also have a surcharge of $30 each way. This was true of most of the domestic airlines we questioned. Air Canada allows one bicycle per passenger with a $15 surcharge. They will provide a bag for $3. Qantas does not have bags or boxes and suggests you purchase one from a domestic airline. They will allow the bicycle as one of two pieces of checked luggage. All bicycles must be checked in one hour before flight time.

Each airline has its own set of rules, and it is best that you explain to the ticketing agent when you make your travel arrangements that you will be bringing a bicycle along as part of your luggage and that you need specific instructions for packing. Repeat all of this when you arrive at the airport and supervise the packing if you want the bike to get there safely.

If you ride the Amtrak rails, you must buy a bike box. The bike is considered part of your luggage, but you should make sure there is baggage service available at your final destination or you won't be able to retrieve the bike when you leave the train.

Greyhound requires a bike box and you can buy one from them at most of their stations. They do not charge an extra fee if the bicycle is checked as part of your luggage.

Chapter 4
Accommodations and Final Plans

Motels and Inns

One of the early decisions you will have to make is whether you want to camp along the road or if you would prefer to stay at a motel or inn and eat at restaurants. This decision will be based not just on your personal preference but also on the route you plan to take. You will need to find out the availability of motels and inns or places to camp along your route. You will also have to consider your budget.

If you plan to stop at motels, be sure to phone ahead well in advance to make reservations and ask about check-in times and closing hours. If you're touring along the Atlantic beaches, you may find the motels and eateries are crowded and expensive. If you would like to stay at a charming inn, read Herbert Hiller's *Guide to the Small and Historic Lodgings of Florida*.

Camping and Cooking

There are 227,492 camp sites in 42 state parks across the state. There are a few campgrounds that are located right on the beaches, especially down in the Keys. If you choose to camp and cook you will find there is a wide variety of camping gear that is both lightweight and compact for you to choose from.

Keep one thing in mind when you start making decisions about what you need to take along for camping: you are going to be providing all the energy to move everything you bring with you. The roomy, comfortable four-man cabin tent will be a little bulky on your handlebars. There are four-man tents which weigh as little as six pounds and will last a lifetime, but they don't come cheap. You might even try out the bivouac sack, which will at least shelter you for the night. For most of your travels in Florida, you can get away with a flannel sheet-blanket instead of a sleeping bag.

A one-burner stove is sufficient for one or two people. Don't carry a lot of food along; it is best to carry no more than a two days' food supply on the bike. You can usually find a store along your route where you can buy food for the night. Stores are also a good place to learn about local customs and get acquainted with local residents.

Again, the bicycle dealer can advise you about the panniers, or packs, to carry your gear. They fit on the bicycle handlebars or over the back wheel. Camping equipment may also be available from your bicycle dealer, or else you can find what you need at one of the large department stores. Below you will find a list of common camping needs. Copy it and check it over carefully before you leave. You won't need everything on the list every trip but checking the list will help you avoid forgetting important items.

Checklist

BICYCLE: You're obviously not going anywhere without your bicycle, but you should take time before each trip to go over the entire bike one more time before you leave. Be sure you have a tire pump fitted on the frame of your bike.

TOOL KIT: Pliers, screwdriver, knife, extra tubes, an emergency flare, and anything else your dealer tells you is necessary.

FIRST-AID KIT: The kit should contain extra personal prescriptions in addition to emergency supplies.

CAMP STOVE: A one-burner unit with disposable fuel cartridges should be adequate.

WATERPROOF MATCHES: These are safer to carry than a cigarette lighter.

COOKING AND EATING SET: The nested pots with plates and eating utensils are a good investment. Don't forget a can opener, paper towels, and a pair of cooking mitts.

DRIED AND CANNED FOODS: It's very awkward to carry a cooler on the handlebars of a bicycle, so you will need foods that don't require cooling.

FLASHLIGHT: Select one that can stand up to rough treatment. Bring extra batteries.

CANDLES: These weigh less than a kerosene lamp or a big flashlight and they don't need fuel or extra batteries.

TENT OR BIVOUAC SACK: Your choice of tent or sack
depends on the time of year and how hardy you are.
Lightweight tents are wonderful but can be expensive.
CLOTHES: Bring what you need but be prudent. Start
with your riding helmet and a cap or scarf to wear when
you're not riding. Then continue down your body to your
footwear. One pair of long pants, shorts, shirts, socks,
underwear, sleepwear, an extra pair of shoes, and rain
gear.
DITTY BAG: Get a waterproof bag for your personal
items such as toothbrush, bar of soap, small sewing kit,
towel, toilet paper, small notebook and pen, extra pre-
scription glasses or sunglasses in a hard case, insect
repellent, personal prescriptions, and suntan lotion.

If you're planning to travel in a group, you might want
to ask someone to accompany you in a car or van. They
can carry all the supplies, food, and camping gear for
everyone. You can ride further and faster without being
loaded down. The car or van that accompanies a group of
riders is referred to as the "sag wagon" because it picks
up riders who sag along the way. The driver can also
travel ahead to set up camp and have a good hot meal
ready when the gang arrives. If your group stays in one
location for a few days, the driver can make some day
trips by bicycle with the group, or you can all take turns
driving the "sag wagon."

Final Plans

When you feel you're ready for your first overnight
ride, go through the complete planning cycle. Begin with
some short weekend trips to check out your stamina and

Photograph by Pat Perdue

your equipment. Take along all the gear on your weekend
trip that you plan to take on the long ride.

Decide how many miles you want to travel in one day
and then try to keep that schedule. Remember you're
supposed to enjoy this trip, so don't try to go too far in
one day. Allow some time for refreshment breaks and
possible equipment breakdowns. Don't forget to make

reservations at the place you plan to stay overnight, just as you would on a long trip.

This first trip will help you determine just how far you can comfortably travel in a day. If you're taking a leisurely scenic trip, you will probably be able to cover 25–30 miles in one day. If you're in top shape and really want to cover some distance, you can make up to 70 miles in a day.

Also, be sure to alert a family member or friend about your trip. Tell them where you're going and where you'll be staying and ask them if they will be close to a phone, just in case you need to be rescued.

When you're ready for the big trip, you must decide if you're going solo, with a friend, or with a group. Next you must decide if you're going to select the route or if you want to go with a tour guide in a group. Finally, you must decide what part of the great state of Florida you want to explore. The location and time of the year are important factors in this decision.

You are now prepared to set off on a wonderful adventure, seeing sights the less fortunate never see from an airplane or a speeding car. All you have to do is decide where to go, and Part Two will help you with that decision. You might want to begin with one of the Florida Bicycle Trails mapped out by the state bicycle program (see pages 69–74). Have a safe and beautiful trip and don't forget to take along your copy of *The Florida Bicycle Book*.

Part Two
On the Road

Photograph courtesy of Dan Burden

A Bicyclist's View of Florida

◆ If you were to measure from the top of the state all the way to the tip of the Florida Keys, you would find that Florida is 447 miles long. Begin in the north and work your way south and you'll discover that Florida is also a state of dramatic contrasts. While glossy travel brochures promote the southern attractions of sandy beaches and stately palm trees, many people are not aware of the special beauty of the northern part of our state.

The fact is, there's much more to Florida than beaches and palm trees. Did you know that almost half the land mass of Florida is covered not with palm trees but with pine trees? Three national forests—the Apalachicola, the Osceola, and the Ocala—cover more than one million acres in north and central Florida. Forestry is big business in our state. The Hudson Paper Company, the Owens-Illinois Corporation, and the St. Regis Corporation own millions of acres in pine tree plantations, spread mostly across the northern regions of the state. Each year thousands of bicycle tourists enjoy the smooth, flat, paved roads that cut through these forests. Imagine miles of quiet, cool riding, with your gear strapped firmly to the handlebars and a bottle of spring water fastened to the frame.

If you begin in north Florida and pedal south, you pass through farm communities like Madison, High Springs, and Newberry. These small towns are surrounded by croplands that were hacked out of wild clumps of palmetto bushes and scrub oaks. At almost every 15-mile intersection, lonely tin-roofed, wide-porched, wood-framed stores sell groceries, livestock feed, gasoline, and hardware. Leather-faced farmers in bib overalls and straw hats stand around the tailgate of a pickup truck and talk in Southern drawls about corn, peanut, and watermelon crops, making you wonder if you really crossed the Georgia line 50 to 100 miles back.

The store is also the local post office and sometimes the Greyhound Bus station, with an air conditioner instead of a potbellied stove to provide comfort. You will be greeted with a "Hey!" for "hello" and can count on "Y'all come back now and see us, ya' hear?" when you leave. And as in any other rural part of the United States, the storekeeper offers free advice and local gossip for as long as you want to sit a spell and listen. In short, if you haven't traveled the back roads of this state, you haven't really seen Florida, and the best way to enjoy the view is on a bicycle.

If, however, you want to head straight for the sandy beaches, you can take U.S. 98 right out of Mobile Bay and travel along the northwestern Gulf Coast of the Panhandle. You can stay overnight in small fishing communities like Sopchoppy, Carrabelle, or Cedar Key. Over on the eastern side of the state, the Atlantic Coast is more populated, but there are more campgrounds and tourist attractions, if you don't mind company.

Just make sure you phone or write ahead for reservations. It can be pretty depressing after a full day of cycling to arrive at a campground that's already full and the next place is 10 miles down the road. The time you take to preplan your trip will be the best investment you can make to assure the success of your trip. And that's what this book is all about—planning and enjoying a trip through the wonders of Florida.

State Bicycle Trails

◆ State bicycle program coordinators at the Florida Department of Transportation and planners from the Department of Natural Resources have spent several years developing a system of bicycle trails that are safe and scenic. On the following pages you will find these trails mapped and described. According to the trail brochure, the trails were designed to introduce you to Florida's best cycling roads. Trained bicycle cartographers mapped these rural roadways with low traffic volumes, good surface conditions, and many scenic or other attractions. This bicycle trail system is made up of 11 loop trails covering a total of 1,220 miles. The trails range from a one-day 30-mile circuit of southeast Florida to a week-long 300-mile trek along the backroads of the

northeast region. Several of these loops can be intercon-
nected to offer up to 500 miles of riding.

Detailed maps for each trail can be obtained by writing or calling either DOT or DNR. The cost is only $1.00
for each set of maps. You can use the form in the back of
this book to order the maps. Note that maps are not yet
available for routes C, I, J, and K.

Florida Bicycle Trails

Route A: Sugar Beaches—Sugar white sand, solitude
and shimmering waters are the setting of this 90-mile
bicycle tour of northeast Florida's beaches. The route
winds through Pensacola, the City of Five Flags, where
restored 18th- and 19th-century buildings preserve the
early influences of the Spanish and English on the Gulf
Islands National Seashore. These white dunes are
graced by sea oats, wax myrtle and wind-pruned scrub
oaks. You will wish you never had to leave.

Route B: Canopy Roads—Ride under a canopy of live
oak trees whose great boughs are draped with Spanish
moss on this 100-mile tour. The route winds through the
history- and tradition-steeped countryside surrounding
Florida's state capital—Tallahassee. Rural roads named
for their destinations climb over the rolling Tallahassee
Hills to historic Monticello, then roll down to the lowlands of the St. Marks River basin where egret and
heron foraging in the shallows are often surprised by alligators. Back in Tallahassee, a tour of the old homes and
the Capitol buildings round out the trip experience.

Route C: Mysterious Waters—This tour also leaves from Tallahassee but follows a southern route to the coast making stops at famous Wakulla Springs, the world's largest spring, the St. Marks National Wildlife Refuge and the small fishing villages of St. Marks and Spring Creek. Wonderful dishes of fresh seafood are served up in these little towns. Be sure to visit them and sample the saltwater delicacies. (Map not yet available.)

Route D: Crystal Springs—Experience the beauty of north central Florida's geological sites as this 100-mile tour reveals clues to Florida's vast underground water system. You begin this journey after visiting the Devil's Millhopper State Geological Site, a giant sinkhole outside of Gainesville. Then, it is on to the clear, bubbling waters of Ginnie Springs. Save a day for tubing down the Ichetucknee River and watch the Santa Fe River disappear at O'Leno State Park. Smoothly paved roads are skirted by grazing pastures and forests and carry you over the gently rolling hills.

Route E: Healing Waters Trail—You can spend a week discovering northeast Florida on this 300-mile tour. Rejuvenate yourself in the waters of this region believed by Juan Ponce De Leon to possess the power of restoring youth. Ponce De Leon came to Florida in search of the Fountain of Youth and gave the state its name "La Florida," or "the land of flowers." Historic sites greet you in this cornerstone of Florida's heritage. Throughout the Ocala National Forest you will follow the trail of 18th-century naturalist William Bartram. A 35-mile ride along the Atlantic Coast brings you to St. Augustine, the

oldest permanent settlement in the nation, where past
and present are intertwined creating an interesting
blend of sights and activities for its visitors.

Route F: Lakes-'n-Hills—This tour covers some 100
miles of central Florida's rolling Central Highlands
which are set with more than 1400 named lakes, offering
a pleasant esape from the tourist spots in this area. The
route winds through the Ocala National Forest to a wildlife refuge and a quiet lakeside recreation area. Mount
Dora, a stopping place on this tour is a quaint resort city
with a New England flavor and many antique shops. This
tour offers many chances to combine bicycling with other
recreational opportunities.

Route G: Withlacoochee Meander—Meander
through the 113,000-acre Withlacoochee State Forest
on this 120-mile bicycle tour of west central Florida.
The Withlacoochee River, one of Florida's best-known
canoe trails, winds through the forest. Stopping points
along the route take advantage of the natural resources
and offer chances for various recreational activities
to enhance the tour experience. In the forest there
are extensive hiking trails and a combination
bicycle/canoeing trip can be arranged with outfitters
on the Withlacoochee River.

Route H: Land O'Lakes—If you have a taste for
adventure and variety, this 155-mile bicycle tour through
the heart of the state is for you. The trail meanders
around the many sparkling lakes of central Florida
where citrus groves form geometric patterns on the

landscape and perfume the air during the blooming season. The trail winds among pastoral hills near some of the state's best-known tourist attractions such as Walt Disney World, Epcot Center, and Sea World.

Route I: Suncoast Highlands — Florida's west coast is known for its beaches and citrus groves but few visitors become acquainted with the "Florida mountains," an area of the state where some elevations reach 200 feet above sea level. This route is a 100-mile tour weaving through the agricultural quilt that blankets these suncoast highlands. Come on this tour with bicycle and body in top shape. (Map not yet available.)

Route J: The Gold Coast — Switching to the attractions of metropolitan south Florida, this region highlights the resources which take advantage of the year-round mild climate. The gardens, parks and animal jungles are among the world's most beautiful, and other attractions give the history of the people who pioneered the exciting Gold Coast. This 30-mile tour covers the flat terrain of the suburban districts of South Miami. (Map not yet available.)

Route K: The Everglades — Miles of sawgrass prairie, occasionally interrupted by pine and hardwood hammock, backdrop most of this 170-mile tour of the tip of Florida. Leaving behind the excitement of the Miami area, you enter the serenity of the over 2,000-square-mile wildlife preserve and begin a 76-mile wilderness journey. Here, tropical life from the Caribbean joins temperate species from the north in one of the largest remaining undisturbed areas of natural habitat in Florida. Sky and land sweep out to the horizon and brown, gold, and green grasses color the earth. Hiking, nature study, and canoeing trips can be arranged with area outfitters. Remember to pack your insect repellent for this tour. (Map not yet available.)

**Florida
Bicycle
Trails**

TRAIL SPECIFICS

KEY	SERVICES						ACCESS			RECREATION						
F—frequent O—occasional R—rare N—none	camping	hotel	restaurant	store	laundry	bike shop	commercial airport	amtrak station	bus station	state park	canoeing	swimming	nature trail	scenic beauty	attractions	total mileage
Route A	F	F	F	F	F	R	X		X			X	X	X	X	90
Route B	R	O	O	F	O	R	X		X	X		X	X	X	X	100
Route C	R	O	O	F	R	R	X		X	X	X	X	X	X	X	145
Route D	F	N	R	O	R	R	X		X	X	X	X	X	X	X	100
Route E	F	F	F	F	O	O	X	X	X	X	X	X	X	X	X	300
Route F	F	O	O	F	R	R	X	X	X	X	X	X	X	X	X	100
Route G	F	O	O	F	O	R	X		X	X	X	X	X	X	X	120
Route H	O	O	O	F	O	R	X	X	X	X		X	X	X	X	155
Route I	O	O	O	O	R	N			X			X	X	X		80
Route J	O	F	F	F	O	O	X	X	X	X		X	X	X	X	30
Route K	O	R	R	R	R	R	X	X	X		X	X	X	X	X	170

The Florida
Rails-to-Trails Program

◆The DNR survey mentioned at the beginning of Part
One concluded there are a growing number of people
who use the bicycle to seek out scenic, educational, and
spiritual values of the outdoors. In response, the state is
working to provide an extensive system of designated
and properly marked routes to afford variety and link
points of origin and destination. With the coordination of
DNR, Florida is also working with regional and local
government agencies to meet the needs of bicyclists.

The state has also become affiliated with the Rails-to-
Trails Conservancy, a national organization founded to
recover abandoned railroad right-of-ways for use as recreational trails for hikers, bicyclists, and horseback
riders. The conservancy publishes a quarterly newslet-
ter; their address is listed in the Appendix.

The Florida Rails-to-Trails program currently is com-
prised of one completed pathway and two pathways
under development, for a total of 61 miles. The completed
pathway is 16.5 miles long and runs from Tallahassee to
St. Marks. The route is an eight-foot wide paved pathway used by hikers, bicycle riders, and horseback riders.

The two pathways under development include a pathway in Alachua County from Gainesville to Hawthorne
just north of Payne's Prairie, and a pathway that runs
along U.S. 41 south from Inverness to the southern
boundary of Citrus County, passing through Fort Cooper
State Park, Floral Park, and the Withlacoochee State

Forest. Detailed information on all Rails-to-Trails paths can be obtained by contacting the Office of Policy and Planning at DNR (see Appendix).

Bicycling in the Eleven Regions of Florida

◆ The Florida Department of Natural Resources divides the state into 11 planning regions. In the sections that follow, we're going to use DNR's boundaries to acquaint you with the varied types of bicycling experiences in store for you in the different regions.

FLORIDA ZONED PLANNING MAP

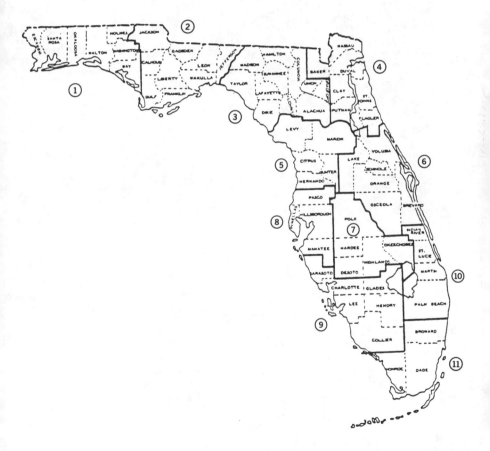

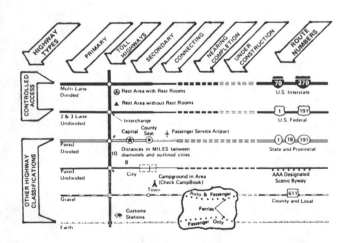

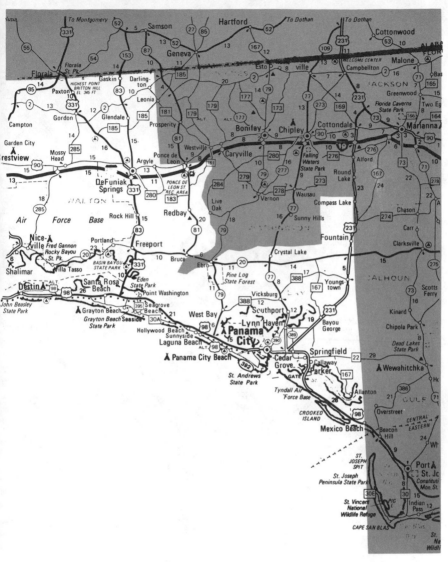

Region 1
Northwest Panhandle

Bay, Escambia, Holmes, Okaloosa, Santa
Rosa, Walton, and Washington counties

Region 1
Northwest Panhandle

◆Florida's Panhandle begins in the northwest corner of the state where the Alabama, Georgia, and Florida borders converge. While many tourists prefer to vacation further south, bicycle riders may find the Panhandle's quiet country roads just to their liking. After all, "If you live in the most perfect place in the world, there's no reason to travel any further," say some of the local residents. If you choose to begin your bicycle tour in the northwest corner of the state, you may find yourself agreeing with them.

Route A of the state bicycle trails program lies in this region and offers a delightful beach tour. Or you may just want to follow U.S. 90 from Mobile Bay, across the corner of Alabama into Florida, and pedal past miles of peanut and watermelon cropland. You can also head on down to U.S. 98 along the Gulf of Mexico and enjoy 100 miles of pure white sandy beaches.

Summertime temperatures hover around 80 degrees and seldom dip below 40 in the winter. The terrain is mostly flat, with a few rolling hills. On U.S. 98 along the Gulf, you'll find plenty of public parks for camping, swimming, fishing, or just having a picnic lunch. Many of the public parks are on the beach, and you can wade out into the Gulf for a half-mile in water that is waist high or take a boat ride out to the offshore islands. Like the locals, you just may not want to go any further south.

MUNICIPAL BICYCLE/
PEDESTRIAN COORDINATOR

Tim Bustos, Pensacola, (904) 444-8910.

BICYCLE CLUBS

The Pensacola Freewheelers Bike Club is an active group and can be contacted by writing to Donald E. Boose, President, 141 Lovett Place, Pensacola, FL 32506, or by calling Jim Fortner at Cycle Source on weekdays—(904) 433-1332. Or contact Sun Wave Velosports, P.O. Box 9058, Pensacola, FL 32513.

BICYCLING EVENTS

The Centurian Rides and the Irish or St. Paddy's Day Ride are both held annually. Write to the Pensacola Freewheelers Bike Club for dates.

STATE BICYCLE TRAILS

Route A: Sugar Beaches Trail—90-mile tour of Florida's northeast beaches (see page 70).

PLACES OF INTEREST

Basin Bayou State Recreation Area sprawls along the spectacular beaches of Choctawhatchee Bay and offers CAMPING, picnicking, hiking, and fishing. The scenery is unusual and rangers offer campfire programs and guided walks. It's located off State Road 20, about 7 miles south of Freeport. (904) 835-3761.

Big Lagoon State Recreation Area is on State Road 292, about 10 miles southwest of Pensacola. There are nature boardwalks and trails, a 500-seat amphi-theater, CAMPING, picnic areas, a pavilion, and the spec-tacular beaches this region is famous for throughout the world. Reserve your campsite well in advance at this popular park. (904) 492-1595.

Blackwater River State Park is located off U.S. 90, about 15 miles northeast of Milton. The river is darkened by the tannic acid from the trees but is one of the cleanest, most pollution-free rivers in the United States. The park is part of the 183,153-acre Blackwater River State Forest. The forest has been preserved in its natural state; no timber removal or cattle grazing is permitted. Visitors can enjoy CAMPING, swimming, canoeing, and hiking. (904) 623-2363.

Eden State Ornamental Gardens are located off U.S. 98 at Point Washington. More than 11 acres of landscaped gardens surround a restored Southern mansion with fireplaces in every room and upstairs and downstairs porches all the way around the house. The house was built by William Henry Wesley in 1898, and the Wesley family lived there until Mrs. Wesley died in 1953. The home is on the banks of Choctawhatchee Bay and was once the center of a large sawmill operation. It was restored by Lois Maxon, a retired New York newspaper reporter, and donated to the state in 1968. The house is open daily from May 1 through September 15 from 9 AM to 4 PM, and you can stop for a picnic in the gardens. (904) 231-4214.

Fred Gannon Rocky Bayou State Recreation Area is about 3 miles east of the town of Niceville. You'll find CAMPING, picnicking, swimming, and fishing. Fred Gannon has 632 acres and is located within the Eglin Air Force Base Reservation. It is jointly managed by state and federal park services. (904) 897-3222.

St. Andrews

State Recreation Area

Grayton Beach State Recreation Area is south of U.S. 98 at the intersection of State Road 283 and State Road 30A. Barrier dunes protect the Western Lake and a nature trail winds through the dunes. CAMPING, picnic pavilions, a bathhouse, and concession stand provide delightful recreation for the visitor. It offers the best of both worlds: a mile of white sandy beach on the Gulf of Mexico and several freshwater lakes are found in this 356-acre state recreation area. (904) 231-4210.

The Gulf Islands National Seashore includes a Spanish fort, San Carlos de Barrancas; the old Pensacola Lighthouse, just south of Pensacola; and Fort Pickens, on the western end of Santa Rosa Island 17 miles offshore from Pensacola. CAMPING, fishing, boating, and swimming are all part of the attractions at this national park.

St. Andrews State Recreation Area is only 3 miles from Panama City on State Road 392. Its 1,063 acres reach out into St. Andrews Bay in the Gulf of Mexico, and you can enjoy CAMPING, picnicking, swimming, boating, fishing, skin diving, nature trails, and a museum. This is one of the most popular state recreation areas in Florida. Rent boats or bicycles at the park office or just enjoy the beach. Campsites are individual, and there is also a barracks with a dining hall available for groups. (904) 234-2522.

Ponce de Leon Springs is the site of a 370-acre state recreation area at the intersection of U.S. 90 and State Road 81, about a half-mile south of the town of Ponce de Leon. Picnicking, swimming, and fishing. (904) 836-4281.

Legend

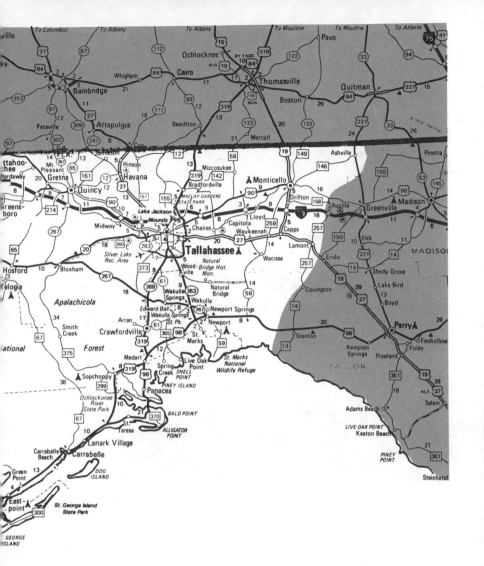

Region 2
Northeast Panhandle

Calhoun, Franklin, Gadsden, Gulf, Jackson, Jefferson, Leon, Liberty, and Wakulla counties

Region 2
Northeast Panhandle

◆During the 1700s, as European settlers moved south and began to establish their cotton plantations, some of the Georgia Creek Indians slipped across the border into Spanish Florida. Traveling mostly in canoes along the Apalachicola River, they joined the remaining Apalachee and Calusa tribes to form a band called Istee Seminolee, a Creek phrase meaning "runaway renegade." It was the beginning of the Seminole Indian Tribe of Florida. While most of the state to the south has been developed and civilized, this part of the state still looks pretty much like it must have back then.

Almost 300 years later, only a few people are permanent residents in this land of pine tree forests and alligator swamps. Small deer, black bears, Florida panthers, and American bald eagles are the primary permanent residents of the northeastern Panhandle region.

Florida's capital is in Tallahassee, the largest city in this region. The original capitol building, which dates back to 1845 when Florida became a state, was threatened with destruction but was saved by a statewide effort. It was carefully restored and a modern, multistory office complex was built around it. The new complex contains the chambers of the House of Representatives and the Senate as well as the governor's offices. The old capitol was refurbished with many of the original furnishings and now houses offices of the legislators.

During the nine months when the legislature is not in session, the city becomes a quiet country town again. The sessions begin in March and end in June. During that time the city celebrates Springtime Tallahassee with art shows, a bicycle race, music festivals, parades, and parties. The whole city blooms with azaleas, camellias, and other flowers of spring.

Also in Tallahassee is Florida State University with a student population of almost 20,000, but they too are temporary residents who head for home every vacation.

MUNICIPAL BICYCLE/ PEDESTRIAN COORDINATOR

Rick Seidel, Tallahassee, (904) 599-8261.

BICYCLE CLUBS

The Capitol City Cyclists group focuses on touring or recreational riding. For information write to Amy Seidler at P.O. Box 4222, Tallahassee, FL 32315, (904) 576-1616. Fat of the Land is a club for mountain bike enthusiasts; the address is 805 Cable Drive, Tallahassee, FL 32301.

BICYCLING EVENTS

The Tour of Tallahassee is held every year in July. There is also an annual tour of the Suwannee River Valley hosted by the Capitol City Cyclists. Don't forget the bicycle race during Springtime Tallahassee. Write to either club for information on these events.

STATE BICYCLE TRAILS

Route B: Canopy Roads—100-mile tour of countryside surrounding Tallahassee (see page 70).

Route C: Mysterious Waters—145-mile tour from Tallahassee to the coast (see page 71).

PLACES OF INTEREST

The Apalachicola National Forest covers more than a half-million acres in Franklin, Liberty, Wakulla, and Leon counties. Because it's so large, it's divided into two management sections. The administrative office for the eastern half of the forest is in Crawfordville on U.S. 319, about 20 miles south of State Road 20. The western administrative offices are in Bristol, west of the Apalachicola River, on State Road 20.

When you cross the Apalachicola River, you also cross into another time zone and must give or take an hour. Three different rivers wind their way through the forest. You'll find stands of planted pines and giant live oak trees, with occasional palm trees adding that Florida tropical look. Boating, picnicking, CAMPING, fishing, and swimming add to the attraction of miles of tree-shaded forest roads to create a bicycling paradise. There are a wide range of camping and recreation facilities within the forest.

Trout Pond Recreation Area for the Handicapped, within the Apalachicola Forest, is unique in the Florida national forests because it is specifically designed for the handicapped. There are no paths in soft sand, no curbs, and no steep trails. All facilities have been modified to meet the needs of those who have difficulty with regular facilities.

Write to the U.S. Forest Service, 214 S. Bronough Street, Tallahassee, FL 32301, for exact information and detailed maps, or call (904) 222-9549.

Constitution Convention State Museum houses dioramas and exhibits of the state's first constitutional

convention in 1839. It's located on U.S. 98 in Port
St. Joe. (904) 229-8029.

Dead Lakes was created when the Apalachicola
River blocked the Chipola River and the water backed
up to form a swamp that killed the trees and vegetation—hence the name "Dead Lakes." This state recreation area is a 41-acre park offering some great fishing,
despite its name. It is located on State Road 71, about
4 miles north of Wewahitchka. CAMPING, boating, and
fishing are available. (904) 639-2702.

Falling Waters State Recreation Area features
an unusual waterfall formed by water flowing from a
sinkhole down through a chimney to an underground cav-
ern. There is a platform overlooking the waterfall for visitors to get a good view. The park is on State Road 77A,
about 3 miles south of Chipley. Visitors can CAMP, swim,
picnic, or hike. (904) 638-4030.

Florida Caverns State Park is loved by spelunkers
who call this place their home away from home. The park

DEAD LAKES STATE RECREATION AREA

covers 1,783 acres off State Road 167, about 3 miles
north of Marianna. Beneath these acres is a vast net-
work of limestone caves. Most Florida caves are below
sea level and are flooded, keeping non-scuba cave explor-
ers out. These caves are small-scale versions of Mam-
moth Caves and contain miles of connecting rooms ready
for exploration. There are also surface trails for hiking,
or you can swim at Blue Hole Springs, where the water
is only 70 degrees on the warmest days. You can also
enjoy CAMPING, fishing, boating, diving, a snack and gift
shop, and picnicking. (904) 482-3632.

Fort Gadsden is a state historic site on State Road
65 north of Apalachicola. The fort is part of a 78-acre
park and was built by the British but occupied by the
Indians. In 1816, American soldiers destroyed the fort
and massacred more than 250 Indian men, women, and
children. Andrew Jackson had the fort rebuilt for American soldiers in 1818. (904) 670-8988.

John Gorrie State Museum honors the man who
invented the first ice-making machine, using ice from a
cooling system designed for malaria patients whom he
cared for in his home. It is located at the intersection of
U.S. 98 and U.S. 319 in downtown Apalachicola. (904)
653-9347.

Lake Jackson Mounds is an 11.5-acre archaeological site on U.S. 27, about 6 miles north of Tallahassee,
where Hernando De Soto spent the winter of 1539–40
with his army and celebrated the first Christmas service
in the United States. It is believed that the Indian
mounds there were once surrounded by an Indian village, probably dating back to 1300 B.C. (904) 562-0042.

Alfred B. Maclay State Ornamental Gardens is 308 acres of ornamental gardens, and the Maclay House museum is on the grounds. The gardens are open only during the blooming season in spring. The gardens are 5 miles north of Tallahassee on U.S. 319. (904) 893-4455.

Natural Bridge Battlefield is an historic site off State Road 363, about 6 miles east of Woodville. A battle was fought there to save Tallahassee from the Federal soldiers, making it the only Southern capital not held by the Union. (904) 925-6216.

Ochlockonee River State Park is also on U.S. 319, about 4 miles south of Sopchoppy. In this 392-acre park, the Dead River converges with the Ochlockonee River and flows into the Gulf of Mexico, 3 miles south. Boat ramps are available and you can catch fresh- and saltwater fish in the area. There are also CAMPING, swimming, and picnicking facilities. (904) 962-2771.

St. George Island State Park is on a barrier island located off the Gulf Coast, sheltering Apalachicola Bay. Here you'll find some of the best oysters in the world. The island is full of sandy coves and salt marshes and covers 1,883 acres. Travel by car is difficult and limited. You can picnic, swim, fish, or hike, but there are no over-night camping facilities available. (904) 670-2111.

San Marcos de Apalache State Historic Site is on State Road 363 near St. Marks National Wildlife Refuge. This 7-acre park is the site of a fort built by the Spanish 300 years ago and captured by Andrew Jackson in 1818. (904) 925-6219.

St. Joseph Peninsula State Park is on County Road 30E or North Beach Street, near Port St. Joe. The T. H. Stone Memorial is located within the boundaries of

the 2,516-acre park. It also features a 20-mile-long beach
with St. Joseph Bay on one side and the Gulf of Mexico
on the other. It's almost completely surrounded by water
and contains small freshwater and saltwater marshes as
well as small freshwater ponds. You can rent a bicycle or
bring your own. CAMPING, picnicking, swimming, fishing, boating, diving, and family cabins make this a great
place to stay a while. (904) 227-1327.

Three Rivers State Recreation Area is near the
Florida-Georgia border. It gets its name from the Flint
and Chattahoochee rivers, which flow together to form
the Apalachicola River below Lake Seminole. The park
offers CAMPING, picnicking, swimming, fishing, and boating on 834 acres. It's on U.S. 90, just 1 mile north of
Sneads. (904) 593-6565.

Torreya State Park is located off State Road 12 on
County Road 271 between Bristol and Greensboro, with
1,063 acres of CAMPING, picnicking, fishing, and hiking
trails which wind through botanical parks. High
bluffs and steep ravines surround the banks of the
Apalachicola River. The Gregory House, an old Southern
mansion, was built at Ocheesee Landing in 1849 and
moved to the park in 1935, piece by piece, by the Civilian Conservation Corps. It is open for tours from 8 A.M.
to sunset. (904) 643-2674.

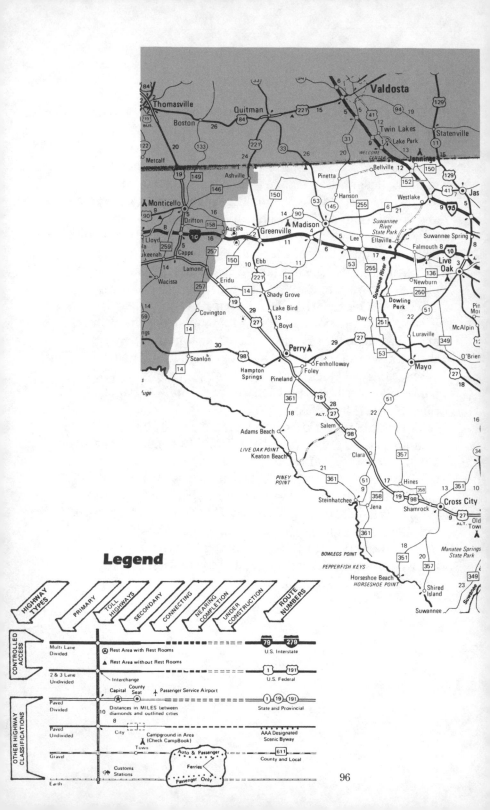

Legend

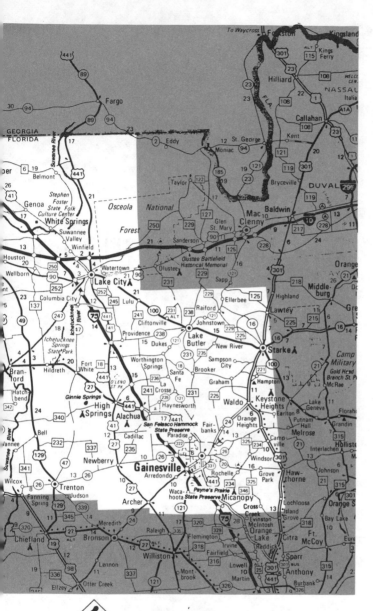

Region 3
North Central Florida

Alachua, Bradford, Columbia, Dixie,
Gilchrist, Hamilton, Lafayette, Madison,
Suwannee, Taylor, and Union counties

Region 3
North Central Florida

◆The Suwannee River originates just north of the Florida-Georgia border in the Okefenokee Swamp. From its
headwaters, the river flows across the state border, then
meanders back and forth across north Florida, picking
its way down to the Gulf of Mexico. While it may not
match the mighty Mississippi in length or breadth, songs
about the Suwannee River have made it fairly well
known. But those songs don't really convey the magic of
the river as it cuts through solid walls of pine tree plantations and the nearest paved road is 30 miles away.
    American Youth Hostels of Florida offers regularly
scheduled bicycle tours in this area. At the present time,
these tours are confined to the Suwannee River and
north Florida regions. In addition to the bicycle tours,
the organization offers overnight and longer canoe trips
on the Suwannee River and other rivers in the area.
There are different schedules for different times of the
year; to get current information, write to the Florida
Council of American Youth Hostels at the address listed
in the Appendix.

MUNICIPAL BICYCLE/
PEDESTRIAN COORDINATOR

    Gainesville—The official coordinator, Mary Ann Koos,
is now in Tallahassee coordinating the state trails program. You can contact Phil Mann at (904) 374-2107 to
obtain a Bicycle Suitability Map for Gainesville. You can
also contact Jerry Tidwell, chairman of the Urban Area
Bicycle Advisory Board, at 2622 NW 28th Place, Gainesville, FL 32605; (904) 372-1157.

BICYCLE CLUBS

The Gainesville Cycling Club: contact Chandler Otis at
Pedalers of Gainesville, 1630 West University Avenue,
Gainesville, FL 32605; (904) 376-5972.

BICYCLING EVENTS

Call the Gainesville Cycling Club.

STATE BICYCLE TRAILS

Route D: Crystal Springs—100-mile tour of several
unusual geological sites, including a giant sinkhole,
Ginnie Springs, and the Ichetucknee River (see page 71).

PLACES OF INTEREST

The Forest Capital State Museum is just south of
Perry in north central Florida on U.S. 27/98/19. The
museum was created to honor one of the major industries
of this region. You'll find it nestled among tall slash pine
in a 14-acre park dotted with picnic tables. It's a spectacular setting and worth stopping to see. The exhibits
are well done and tell the history of forestry in the state.
There is no camping here, but there are several private
campgrounds nearby. (904) 584-3227.

Stephen Foster State Folk Center is off U.S. 441
near White Springs and contains a museum, a carillon
tower, and an amphitheater. Several folk festivals are
held here each year, including the Labor Day weekend
festival where visitors can enjoy bluegrass bands, folk
singers, cloggers, and exhibits of arts and crafts. The
park is not equipped for camping and the nearest camp-

grounds are some distance away, but Suwannee Country Tours can help out on lodging arrangements. (904) 397-2733.

Ichetucknee Springs State Park, about 4 miles northwest of Fort White, is a unique, riverfront park, with tubing the major attraction. Tubing is a little-known sport that requires the placement of your body inside an old tire inner tube and the launching of your body, in the tube, into ice-cold, spring-fed water for a 3.5-mile float downriver—great fun on a hot sunny day. There's no food or drink allowed on the trip, and the river bottom and banks are so clean and clear that even in depths of 12–15 feet, you can see the rocks and marine life along the bottom. Scuba or skin diving is spectacular. Rent or bring your own inner tubes. At the take-out point on County Road 137, west of Fort White, a shuttle bus will take you back to your bicycle. Try to make the trip on a weekday because on a hot Sunday in July the river looks like a major freeway—not bumper-to-bumper, but tuber-to-tuber. There are no camping facilities in the park, but private campgrounds are very close by. (904) 497-2511.

O'Leno State Park on U.S. 41 near Lake Butler covers 5,898 acres. The Santa Fe River goes underground within the park and surfaces again several miles away. You can CAMP, picnic, swim, or fish, and there are cabins available for groups to rent. (904) 454-1853.

Payne's Prairie State Preserve is an 18,000-acre preserve south of Gainesville on U.S. 441 and I-75. It is believed that this entire area was once covered by a lake. The town of Micanopy at the southern edge of the preserve has a monument to Seminole Chief Micanopy. Many

legends have sprung from the fighting here during the
Seminole Wars. (904) 466-3397.

Marjorie Kinnan Rawlings Museum is the former
home of the woman who wrote *The Yearling* and *Cross
Creek*. Her rustic frame house has been preserved as a
museum. It is located on U.S. 325 (21 miles southeast of
Gainesville). There is a small park where you can picnic.
(904) 466-3672.

San Felasco Hammock State Preserve offers visitors an opportunity to view an incredible Florida sinkhole firsthand. Sinkholes are formed by underground
water erosion around the buried limestone deposits. The
preserve covers 5,461 acres and is about 4 miles northwest of Gainesville, on State Road 232. Rangers provide
guided tours of the rare plants and prehistoric and historic Indian sites. (904) 377-5935.

Legend

Region 4
Northeast Florida

Baker, Clay, Duval, Flagler, Nassau, Putnam and St. Johns counties

Region 4
Northeast Florida

◆ Visitors from many eastern states travel down State
Road A1A into Florida, following the coastline of the
Atlantic Ocean. Like the Gulf Coast in the western Panhandle, the Atlantic Coast features campgrounds and
tourist attractions and the living is easy, if somewhat
more costly.

Many Florida snowbirds are content to end their
southern migration in Jacksonville or St. Augustine.
Jacksonville is a thriving city with a busy port and several military installations. It is the only area in the state
where the entire county is within the city limits and is
governed by the city.

St. Augustine was the first official city in the United
States. Ponce de Leon landed here in 1521 in his search
for the fountain of youth, and the city is a place of wonder for history buffs. Castillo de San Marcos, the country's oldest masonry fort, on St. Augustine Beach, is
still guarded by cannons. Nowadays they are fired in the
evening to entertain, rather than for their more deadly
original purpose. Osceola, warrior chief of the Florida
Seminole Indians, was once held captive at the fort during the Seminole War of 1836. The "world's smallest
schoolhouse" and Ripley's Museum offer visitors both
history and entertainment. St. Augustine is also the
home of Florida's troubadour, Gamble Rogers. His songs
about famous Floridians are heard at folk festivals
around the world. You can spend an evening at a local
pub and enjoy his lively entertainment when he's not out
on tour.

A few miles inland are dairy and potato farms. The
rich loamy soil is distinctly different from the sandy soil a

little further south. The farms are bordered by the Osceola National Forest, where bicycle tourists can enjoy cool and quiet riding and some great fishing holes.

MUNICIPAL BICYCLE/ PEDESTRIAN COORDINATOR

Lee Smith, Jacksonville, (904) 630-1903.

BICYCLE CLUBS

The North Florida Bicycle Club at P.O. Box 14294, Jacksonville, FL 32238; (904) 636-0419. The Rural Bicycle Association, Box 610, Interlachen, FL 32048. Arlington Bicycle Club, 1025 Arlington Road, Jacksonville, FL 32211; (904) 724-4922. St. Augustine Bicycle Club, 58½ San Marco Avenue, St. Augustine, FL 33734; contact Thom Thaldorf (904) 797-6423.

STATE BICYCLE TRAILS

Route E: Healing Waters Trail—Starts at the Fountain of Youth spring in St. Augustine and covers 300 miles down through the Ocala National Forest (see pages 71–72).

PLACES OF INTEREST

ANASTASIA
state recreation area

Anastasia Island Recreation Area on State Road A1A offers secluded CAMPING, picnicking, diving, fishing and boating. It is across the Matanzas River from historic St. Augustine. Here you'll find the place where the Spanish dug their coquina shells to build the fort Castillo de San Marcos. The campsites are kindly located in a shaded area and the swimming pool is the Atlantic Ocean. It's a great place to spend several days while you sightsee around the area. (904) 471-3033.

Bulow Plantation Ruins State Historic Site on State Road 5A southeast of Bunnell covers 109 acres and marks the site of a 6,000-acre plantation that was destroyed during the Seminole War of 1835. The remains of a sugar mill and springhouse and the foundation of the mansion are all that is left. (904) 439-2219.

Faver-Dykes State Park is off U.S. 1 along the Matanzas River and Pelican Creek, 15 miles south of St. Augustine. This 752-acre park offers CAMPING, hiking, picnicking, fishing, and boating. (904) 794-0997.

Flagler Beach State Recreation Area is the snowbird's dream park. It offers 145 acres of CAMPING on the beaches of the Atlantic Ocean, with swimming, boating, diving, and picnicking. Pelicans fish just offshore, the Florida scrub jay nests here, and the giant sea turtles lay their eggs along this beach. A nature trail takes you through the marsh where many species of birds spend their winters. Take State Road A1A 3 miles south of the town of Flagler Beach. (904) 439-2474.

Fort Clinch State Park on Amelia Island is the site of a fort built by the United States to guard the passage of ships through Cumberland Sound during the Civil War. The fort was captured by the Confederates before it was completed in 1861 and was retaken by Union soldiers in 1862. It was also used during the Spanish-American War and briefly during World War II. It is located at the state line off State Road A1A, about 3 miles from Fernandina Beach. Enjoy CAMPING, diving, swimming, picnicking, guided tours, and a snack bar. (904) 261-4212.

Kingsley Plantation is a historic site at Fort George Island off State Road A1A with a restored plantation house and picnic facilities. (904) 251-3122.

Little Talbot Island State Park has boundary lines that have changed dramatically over the years. The forces of wind, water, and shifting sands change the shape of this island constantly. It is surrounded by the Atlantic Ocean, the Fort George River, and Nassau

Sound and offers 2,500 acres of Atlantic beach CAMPING, swimming, picnicking, fishing, boating and diving. The park is about 17 miles northeast of Jacksonville on State Road A1A. (904) 251-3231.

Gold Head Branch State Park is a unique site located northeast of Keystone Heights on State Road 21. Springs tumble forth from the side of ravines to form the Gold Head Branch stream that empties into Lake Johnson. The park covers 1,481 acres and offers full-service and primitive CAMPING, swimming in several lakes, diving, picnicking, a snack shop, and cottages to rent. (904) 473-4701.

Olustee Battlefield Historic Site is a 270-acre state park on U.S. 90 about 2 miles east of Olustee. It was the site of the biggest Civil War battle in Florida. (904) 752-3866.

Ravine State Ornamental Garden, on Twigg Street in Palatka, features azaleas and other ornamental plants. The gardens surround the civic center and offer miles of walking trails. (904) 328-4366.

Washington Oaks State Ornamental Garden is 3 miles south of Marineland on State Road A1A and covers 341 acres. There is a museum, a visitor's center, fishing, picnicking, and miles of trails surrounding the civic center. (904) 445-3161.

Legend

HIGHWAY TYPES — PRIMARY, TOLL HIGHWAYS, SECONDARY, CONNECTING, NEARING COMPLETION, UNDER CONSTRUCTION, ROUTE NUMBERS

CONTROLLED ACCESS

Multi-Lane Divided

Ⓐ Rest Area with Rest Rooms
▲ Rest Area without Rest Rooms

〔79〕 〔279〕 U.S. Interstate

2 & 3 Lane Undivided

Interchange

〔1〕 〔191〕 U.S. Federal

OTHER HIGHWAY CLASSIFICATIONS

Paved Divided

✪ Capital
◉ County Seat
✈ Passenger Service Airport

〔1〕〔19〕〔191〕 State and Provincial

Distances in MILES between diamonds and outlined cities

Paved Undivided

City

▲ Campground in Area (Check CampBook)

AAA Designated Scenic Byway

Town

Gravel

Auto & Passenger
Ferries
Passenger Only

〔611〕 County and Local

⚓ Customs Stations

Earth

112

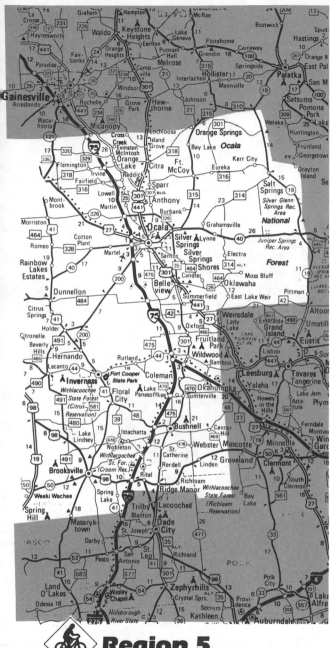

West Central Florida

Citrus, Hernando, Levy, Marion, and Sumter counties

Region 5
West Central Florida

◆ Thundering hoofbeats break the springtime early
morning silence as thoroughbred mares are turned out
with their new foals to take their morning gallops at the
stud farms in Marion County. The Florida horse breeding industry may not yet have the reputation of the bluegrass farms of Kentucky, but it's growing by leaps and
bounds. More horsemen are moving their breeding oper-
ations to the Ocala area every year. Phosphate deposits
enrich the soil for better year-round grazing, and warm
weather means colts and fillies enter the world in January instead of March or April, giving them an advantage
when they begin their careers at the track. One of the
many farms that nestle among the Marion County hills
belongs to New York Yankees owner George Steinbren-
ner, a prime promoter of the Florida racing industry.

MUNICIPAL BICYCLE/
PEDESTRIAN COORDINATOR

None at this time.

BICYCLE CLUBS

Ocala Cycling Club, P.O. Box 6036, Ocala, FL 32678.
Ocala Mountain Bike Club, c/o Ocala Motocross Park,
6849 Gainesville Road, Ocala, FL 32675; contact Laura
Perry (904) 622-5269.

STATE BICYCLE TRAILS

Route G: Withlacoochee Meander—130 miles through
the Withlacoochee State Forest (see page 72).

PLACES OF INTEREST

Ocala National Forest is the southernmost national forest in the continental United States. Covering more than 350,000 acres, the subtropical vegetation is unique to this forest. Scattered throughout the forest are small lakes for fishing, streams for canoeing, and CAMPING in full-service and primitive campsites. Salt Springs is a favorite campground, and the Florida Hiking Trail winds through the forest. There are small, clear lakes with white sandy bottoms that look as though you could just walk across them. But many of them are 15 to 20 feet deep and often closely guarded by alligator families. It's not a good idea to swim alone in these lakes but spectacular if you have someone to keep watch against toothy visitors. (904) 685-2048.

Cedar Key State Museum is in the Gulf Coast fishing village and artists' colony of Cedar Key. An art festival is held here each year in May, and the shrimp fleet brings fresh seafood daily to the many fine restaurants in this out-of-the-way village. Cedar Key is on State Road 24, about 30 miles west of State Road 98 at Otter Creek. (904) 543-5350.

Crystal River Archaeological Site is off U.S. 19/ 98 in Crystal River. This is a pre-Columbian dig surrounded by a 14-acre park. Of the 450 grave sites uncovered, several contained artifacts indicating the graves were those of Indians who lived in the Ohio River Valley 1,600 years ago. A museum allows visitors to view preserved burial mounds, and you can follow trails through the park to view other mounds. (904) 795-3817.

FORT   COOPER
STATE   PARK

Dade Battlefield Historic Site was the scene of a major battle during the Seminole War of 1835. A company of U.S. soldiers, led by Major Francis Dade, was ambushed on the Fort King Military Road and nearly 100 men were killed. There is a memorial and museum where visitors can hear the history of this war from both the U.S. and the Seminole point of view. The battle is reenacted each year in December by volunteers dressed as U.S. Army soldiers of 1835 and Seminole Indians, whose traditional clothing is still worn by most of the tribe members today. There is picnicking, a playground, tennis, the museum, and nature trails at the 80-acre park on U.S. 301 in Bushnell. (904) 793-4781.

Fort Cooper State Park is the site of a fort built during the Seminole Wars to provide shelter for General Winfield Scott's wounded troops during a retreat following their defeat by the Seminoles. The fort was occupied only for about 16 days while the soldiers waited for res-

cue. Fort Cooper Day is held each year in May to com-
memorate the battles there. Covering 704 acres on the
banks of Lake Holathlikaha, the park offers swimming,
canoes, fishing, and primitive CAMPING. (904) 726-0315.

Manatee Springs State Park is 6 miles west of
Chiefland on State Road 320 and covers 2,074 acres. The
springs pump out 116 million gallons of cold, clear water
daily, and an attractive swimming area surrounds them.
This a great place to camp and spend some time diving.
There are picnic pavilions; boat, canoe, and bicycle
rentals; CAMPING; and a snack bar. (904) 493-4288.

In addition to the Ocala National Forest, Region 5 also
features **Withlacoochee State Forest.** The Green
Swamp contained within this area gives birth to the
Withlacoochee River, which cuts through the forest and
is a favorite of canoe campers. Many CAMPING sites line
the river banks, including the Silver Lake Campgrounds
reached by car or canoe. It is not as accessible by bicycle
but worth the trip if you have time to stay a few days.

Wacasassa Bay State Preserve is the reward for
bicycle riders who choose to pedal the long highway to
Cedar Key on State Road 24. CAMPING is primitive but
spectacular. It is accessible only by boat, and there is a
ferry service maintained by the park service. You can
arrange to leave your bicycle in the safekeeping of the
park officers. (904) 543-5567.

Yulee Sugar Mill Ruins Historic Site is located
on County Road 490 in Homosassa. David Levy Yulee, a
U.S. senator from Florida, had dreams of making sugar
cane a major crop and source of income for the state.
All that remains is the ruins of the mill, built in 1851.
(904) 795-3817.

Legend

HIGHWAY TYPES | **PRIMARY** | **TOLL HIGHWAYS** | **SECONDARY** | **CONNECTING** | **NEARING COMPLETION** | **UNDER CONSTRUCTION** | **ROUTE NUMBERS**

CONTROLLED ACCESS		
Multi-Lane Divided	® Rest Area with Rest Rooms	79 279 U.S. Interstate
2 & 3 Lane Undivided	▲ Rest Area without Rest Rooms	1 191 U.S. Federal

Interchange

Capital County Seat ✈ Passenger Service Airport

OTHER HIGHWAY CLASSIFICATIONS		
Paved Divided	Distances in MILES between diamonds and outlined cities 10 8	1 19 191 State and Provincial
Paved Undivided	City Campground in Area (Check CampBook)	611 AAA Designated Scenic Byway
Gravel	Town Auto & Passenger Ferries	County and Local
Earth	⚓ Customs Stations Passenger Only	

State Park

State Park

Ormond Beach ⅄
Holly Hill
Daytona Beach ⅄
Daytona Beach Shores
South Daytona Beach
Port Orange
Allandale
Oaks
Ponce Inlet
New Smyrna Beach
Sugar Mill Ruins
State Historic Site
New Smyrna Beach ⅄
Edgewater
Eldora

95 15

Canaveral

Oak Hill

18

National

Osceola

Scottsmoor

9

Seashore

Geneva

17

8

Mims

7

46

GOVERNMENT RESERVATION ROAD CLOSED TO PUBLIC

John F. Kennedy Space Center

Chuluota

St. Johns Nat'l. Wildlife Refuge

Titusville

Merritt Island Nat'l. Wildlife Refuge

CANAVERAL PENINSULA

420

14

50

405

Visitors Center

FALSE CAPE ROAD CLOSED

Christmas
Tosohatchee State Preserve

520

407

Courtenay

1

CAPE CANAVERAL

ROAD CLOSED

LINE

18

6

528

9

Cape Canaveral ⅄

6

524

8

Merritt Island

10

Cocoa

Georgiana

Cocoa Beach

532

Rockledge

10

Lotus

Patrick Air Force Base (Missile Test Center)

532 21

13

419

10

Tropic

A1A

Satellite Beach
Indian Harbour Beach

192

Holopaw

511 10

13

192

12

Eau Gallie

Melbourne **Indialantic**
Melbourne Beach ⅄

Deer Park

W. Melbourne

6

Palm Bay

21

Port Malabar

514

Malabar

4

Valkaria

Floridana Beach

441

FLORIDA'S

Kenansville

Grant

1

Micco

Sebastian Inlet State Park

Barefoot Bay
Roseland ⅄
Sebastian ⅄

26

28

Pelican Island Wilderness

14

Fellsmere

507

912

510

Wabasso
Winter Beach
Indian River
Gifford Shores

512

505

ALT

630

Riomar

INDIAN RIVER

Vero Beach ⅄

Osio

606

Yeehaw Jct.

60

23

8

607

95

614

Fort Pierce Inlet State Rec. Area

20

41

TPK.

9

Indian

St. Lucie

713

Pierce Inlet

Ft. Drum

BREVARD

Region 6
East Central

Brevard, Lake, Orange, Osceola, Seminole, and Volusia counties

Region 6
East Central

◆ The Orlando area is the tourist center of Florida, offering places to see and things to do that could fill many months. This is the part of Florida where Mickey Mouse lives when he's not in California or Japan. To the west along the coast are Cape Canaveral and the Kennedy Space Center. The problem is that few of the attractions make any provisions for bicycle tourists who might want to leave their bicycles and gear in a safe place while they take in the entertainment. When you are touring this area by bicycle, you should check into a hotel or campground where transportation is provided to all the main attractions including Epcot Center, Disney World, Sea World, and all the rest. We were assured by several theme parks that as the number of bicycle tourists increases, more provisions will be made for them.

This is also that section of Florida that catches a fever every year in February as the cool air heats up with the smell of exotic fuels and the sound of high-powered engines tuning up for the Daytona 500 stock car races, which kick off the major stock car racing season. They have something in Daytona Beach called Speed Week and it brings in bigger crowds every year. The only way to get around Daytona with ease during that time is on a bicycle.

But through the middle of this region you can still find serene country roads that wind around some of the most beautiful small lakes in the state. Leesburg even offers some gentle hills to puff up and down. You will ride through orange groves that seem to stretch for miles. Ride this route in early spring and the smell of orange blossoms in the air will make you want to stop and inhale great gulps of this heavenly scent.

MUNICIPAL BICYCLE/ PEDESTRIAN COORDINATOR

Barbara Meyer, Merritt Island, (407) 453-9518.

BICYCLE CLUBS

DeLand Bicycle Club, P.O. Box 1268, DeLand, FL 32720. Florida Freewheelers, Inc., P.O. Box 547201, Orlando, FL 32854; contact David Salvadorini (407) 695-8486 or (407) 774-5561. West Volusia Wheelmen, c/o J. Mancuso, 1317 Voorhis, DeLand, FL 32720. Spacecoast Freewheelers, c/o Irvin Hayes, 166A N. Atlantic Ave., Cocoa Beach, FL 32931. Mount Dora Cycling Club, 250 Donnelly St., Mount Dora, FL 32757; (904) 735-0155. Halifax Bicycle Touring Club, P.O. Box 173, Ormond Beach, FL 32074. Gator Raiders, Jody Butterworth, (407) 582-3279.

STATE BICYCLE TRAILS

Route F: Lakes-'n-Hills—100 miles of meandering through the hilly lake country of central Florida (see page 72).

PLACES OF INTEREST

Blue Springs State Park is a 945-acre park about 6 miles south of DeLand on U.S. 17/92. When naturalist and author John Bartram traveled this area along the St. Johns River in 1766, he discovered creatures in the

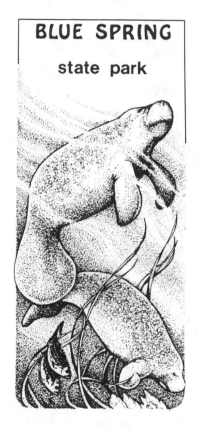

BLUE SPRING

state park

waters that he was sure were mermaids. Today we know these creatures as manatees and they gather in Blue Spring Run every winter. They are on the endangered species list and are definitely worth seeing. Blue Springs contains facilities for CAMPING, picnics, swimming, fishing, boat rentals, and a snack bar. (904) 775-3663.

Hontoon Island State Park is right next door to Blue Springs and is administered by the same park office. Reached only by boat, there is a free ferryboat ride from 9 A.M. to one hour before sundown. No vehicles except bicycles are allowed on the island. Artifacts of the Timucuan Indians dating back to 600 B.C. have been found here in a large Indian mound. The 1,650-acre Hontoon Island is a bald eagle sanctuary; an observation tower gives visitors a 20-mile view in all directions. There is CAMPING, picnicking, fishing, cottages, a snack bar, and bicycle rentals, making this a great bicyclists' vacation spot.

Located off U.S. 17/92 about 6 miles south of DeLand. (904) 734-7158.

Lake Griffin State Recreation Area is on the edge of Lake Griffin, one of the largest lakes in the center of the state along the central ridge of Florida. The Oklawaha River flows north from the lake, eventually reaching the northward-flowing St. Johns River. Located 3 miles north of Leesburg on U.S. 27/441, the area covers 423 acres where visitors can enjoy CAMPING, picnicking, fishing, boating, and canoe rentals. (904) 787-7402.

Lake Louisa State Park is 7 miles south of Clermont and is one of the best-kept secrets in Florida. Follow State Road 50 out of Clermont to County Road 561 and turn left on Lake Nellie Road. There you can enjoy nature trails, swimming, fishing, picnicking, and the breathtaking beauty of this lake. It is seldom crowded and bicycle riders will enjoy the quiet serenity of this park. (904) 394-2280.

New Smyrna Beach Sugar Mill Ruins State Historic Site is similar to the Yulee Sugar Mill near Homosassa (in Region 5) and was also destroyed during the Seminole Wars. It's located on State Road 44 west of U.S. 1 in New Smyrna Beach and contains 17 acres. (904) 428-2126.

Tomoka State Park, about 3 miles north of Ormond Beach on Beach Street, offers 915 acres with CAMPING, hiking, picnicking, fishing, boating, canoe rentals, a museum, gift shop, and snack bar. The Halifax and Tomoka rivers converge in this park to form a sheltered lagoon where the Nocoroco Timucuan Indian Village once stood. The Indians believed the waters were blessed and could cure illnesses. At the very least they are great for curing tired, aching muscles after a long bike ride. (904) 677-3931.

Tosohatchee State Reserve is 28,000 acres of woodlands and wetlands along the St. Johns River. The reserve is a floodplain and water storage and cleaning area for the river. The park contains Indian mounds and offers primitive CAMPING, hiking, fishing, and limited hunting. It is on Taylor Creek Road, about 4 miles south of State Road 50 at Christmas, Florida. The admonition "Don't feed the alligators" is especially true in this park. (305) 568-5893.

Wekiwa Springs State Park covers 6,396 acres and is one of Florida's largest state parks. It is located off State Road 436, about 3 miles east of Apopka, and contains vast expanses of open forest and jungle-like areas. You can swim, fish, picnic, boat, and hike, and there are primitive CAMPING sites as well as cabins available for rental by groups. (305) 889-3140.

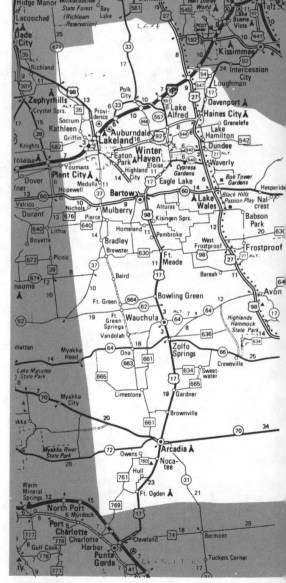

Region 7
Central Florida

DeSoto, Hardee, Highlands, Okeechobee, and Polk counties

Legend

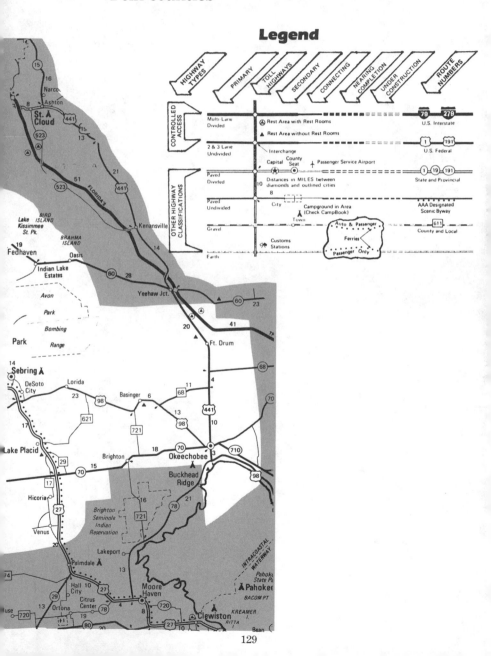

Region 7
Central Florida

◆ Cattle ranches, citrus groves, and phosphate mines
sprawl across this region of Florida. It is different from
the coastal areas, with some rolling hills to challenge a
rider.

North of Clermont at Lake Wales on U.S. 441, atop
one of the highest hills—290-foot Iron Mountain—is the
Bok Singing Tower built by philanthropist Edward Bok.
A 53-bell carillon is mounted on a 205-foot tower of Florida coquina shells and Georgia marble, and each day at 3
P.M. the bells ring out in a 45-minute concert. The 117-
acre Bok Tower Gardens surround the tower and provide
a quiet sanctuary for people to enjoy. One of the highlights of the year is the Easter sunrise service held here
annually.

South of Lake Wales about 2 miles is an amphitheater
where the Black Hills Passion Play is presented about
five times a week during the Lenten season. The director of the company is a seventh-generation Passion Play
actor. The original, permanent home of the company is in
Spearfish, South Dakota, but like many other snowbirds,
its members come south every winter.

The high points of the year in Okeechobee County
near Yeehaw Junction include the Speckled Perch Festival in March and the Labor Day Weekend Cattlemen's
Rodeo. On the northern edge of Lake Okeechobee, the
Brighton Seminole Indian Reservation welcomes visitors
to an annual fair and rodeo in April.

At the intersection of U.S. 27/98 and I-4, you'll find
Baseball City, where several major league baseball
teams hold their spring training. Cypress Gardens,
south of Winter Haven, was started in the 1930s and has

improved year after year. There are year-round exhibits of tropical flowers and ski shows. Recently, a cinema, a children's funland, and gift shops have been added. Many campgrounds have been built through these hills, and they provide daily bus tours to Disney, Sea World and the other local attractions.

The city of Lakeland was once a sleepy farm community containing 13 lakes within the city limits. Located at I-4 and the junction of U.S. 98 and U.S. 92, about halfway between Tampa and Orlando, it has become the home of many new manufacturing plants and warehouses. The Lakeland Civic Center was built in 1974 and hosts rock concerts, circuses, rodeos, and trade shows.

In the center of DeSoto County is the town of Arcadia, known for two annual rodeos which draw thousands of spectators each March and July. During the festivities, local cowboys on horseback ride through a bar and "shoot" into the ceiling. Sometimes shoot-outs are enacted, complete with bar maids, deputies, bad guys and hangings. Visitors also can see some examples of Victorian and old Florida architecture in the homes on Arcadia's tree-lined streets. The area's economy is based on cattle ranching and citrus groves.

But for most of your travels in this central heartland, you can pedal for miles and see nothing but cows and citrus trees.

MUNICIPAL BICYCLE/ PEDESTRIAN COORDINATOR

Joanna Hoit, Bartow, (813) 534-6000

BICYCLE CLUBS

Polk Area Bicycling Association, 5100 St. Lucia Drive,
Lakeland, FL 33813; contact Bob Edwards (813) 646-
4845. Pedal Power Velo Sport, 1058 South Florida Avenue, Lakeland, FL 33803.

STATE BICYCLE TRAILS

Route H: Land O'Lakes—155-mile route through
orange groves and past sparkling lakes (see pages
72–73).

PLACES OF INTEREST

Highlands Hammock State Park was established
to preserve a stand of tropical hardwood trees. The
small Florida deer, alligators, otters, and panthers prowl
among 3,800 acres of scrub palmettos beneath the
orchids and air plants. Visitors can take tours on the
boardwalks or on the train, and there is CAMPING, picnicking, fishing, bicycle rentals, and a snack bar at this
lush Florida park off U.S. 27, about 6 miles west of Sebr-
ing. (813) 385-0011.

LAKE KISSIMMEE
State Park

Lake Kissimmee State Park is 15 miles east of Lake Wales, off Camp Mack Road, and offers swimming, CAMPING, fishing and nature trails. The park covers 5,030 acres and is bordered by Lake Kissimmee, Lake Tiger, and Lake Rosalie. The Kissimmee River, according to Indian legend, was formed when a young Seminole brave ate forbidden food and was turned into a giant snake. He slithered down through the south Florida marshlands to Lake Okeechobee, and the path he left formed the Kissimmee River. At one time the Kissimmee River was rerouted by the Army Corps of Engineers, but the state is now undertaking the removal of the dams and the restoration of the natural wetlands in this area. This is a fisherman's paradise and offers hiking and primitive CAMPING to hardy visitors. The state maintains the Kissimmee Cow Camp in this park and offers a living history program where park rangers reenact the life of the old Florida cow hunters setting out on a cattle drive. (813) 696-1112.

Prairie Lakes State Preserve is about 14 miles
north of Yeehaw Junction on U.S. 441 and 10 miles west
of Kenanville on State Road 523. There is a picnic area,
fishing, and nature trails. (305) 436-1626.

Region 8
Gulf Coast

Hillsborough, Manatee, Pasco, and Pinellas counties

Legend

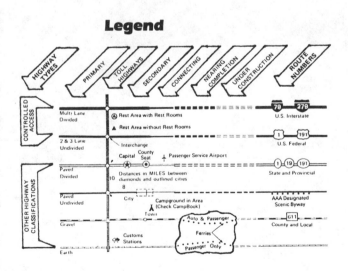

Region 8
Gulf Coast

◆ From Tarpon Springs, home of the Greek sponge fish-
ermen, to the Longboat Key captains who operate fleets
of charter fishing boats, the warmth of the people along
Florida's Gulf Coast attracts more visitors every year.
Out-of-state visitors who once vacationed in Miami have
begun to discover the softer surf and white sands of the
Gulf of Mexico.

However, the serene beauty of Florida's Gulf Coast is
rapidly changing with the influx of more and more permanent residents and is in danger of becoming a mega-
lopolis. The everyday living is so attractive that several
major corporations have moved their headquarters into
the Tampa and St. Petersburg areas. High-tech busi-
nesses find the low-cost labor and tax incentives the perfect setting for their new enterprises to flourish.
Highway construction has not kept up with this growth,
and bicycle riding in the heavily populated areas should
be confined to trails or club rides.

There are several bicycle clubs in this area, including a
very active group at the University of South Florida in
Tampa. They offer weekend rides, big-purse races,
triathlons, and family fun rides. Bicycling is not permitted on the beaches, but you can enjoy a beach party
cookout while watching the sunset across the Gulf of
Mexico and think about staying forever.

MUNICIPAL BICYCLE/
PEDESTRIAN COORDINATOR

Ned Baier, Clearwater, (813) 462-4751; Dennis Scott,
Tampa, (813) 272-5940.

BICYCLE CLUBS

Tampa Bay Freewheeler, P.O. Box 8081, Tampa, FL
33674; (813) 933-2431. Tampa Bay Bicycle Sport, P.O.
Box 5152, Clearwater, FL 33518; contact Dennis Tipton
(813) 938-5691. St. Petersburg Bicycle Club, P.O. Box
76023, St. Petersburg, FL 33734; contact Tom Stevenson
(813) 894-7242. University of South Florida Bicycle Club,
P.O. Box CTR 2452, Tampa, FL 33620. Beach Street
Racing, 7517 Blind Pass Road, St. Petersburg, FL
33706; (813) 367-5001.

STATE BICYCLE TRAILS

Route I: Suncoast Highlands—100 miles of hills blan-
keted by agricultural lands (see page 73).

PLACES OF INTEREST

Caladesi Island State Park lies 2 miles off Dunedin
Beach and is accessible only by boat. It is an uncut dia-
mond off the coast of urban growth. Ospreys nest here
and sea turtles lay their eggs beneath the sand. A ferryboat takes visitors out to the 607-acre island where they
can picnic, swim, fish, dive, and hike. You can climb a
60-foot observation tower and view the entire island.
(813) 443-5903.

Gamble Plantation State Historic Site is a 5-acre
estate surrounding the Judah P. Benjamin Confederate
Memorial at Gamble Plantation. The restored mansion,
built in 1845, was part of a sugar plantation that covered
3,500 acres. The walls are two feet thick and made from
oyster shells combined with sand. Built before air condi-

JUDAH P. BENJAMIN CONFEDERATE
MEMORIAL at

GAMBLE   PLANTATION   STATE
HISTORIC SITE

tioning, the construction was designed to keep the owners cool in the hot Florida summers. Picnic sites and
guided tours are available. Located on U.S. 301 near
Ellenton. (813) 722-1017.

Hillsborough River State Park is a 2,964-acre
park on the banks of the Hillsborough River on U.S. 301,
about 6 miles south of Zephyrhills and about 15 miles
north of Tampa. The park was developed by the Civilian
Conservation Corps in 1936. Park rangers offer guided
tours and campfire programs. You'll find everything a
park should have here, including CAMPING, swimming,
hiking, fishing, boating, canoe or paddle boat rentals,
and a snack bar. (813) 986-1020.

Fort Foster Historical Site is maintained by the
Hillsborough River State Park staff and is located across
U.S. 301 from the park. The fort was built during the
Seminole Wars of 1835 to protect the bridge over the
river along the Fort King Military Trail. It was rebuilt in
1980 on the original site using drawings and plans from

the original construction. Volunteers dressed in uniforms of the period man the fort on weekends, and visitors are taken back to 1835 by soldiers who pretend they are still living through the battles with the Seminole Indians. (813) 986-1020.

Lake Manatee State Recreation Area is 14 miles east of Bradenton on State Road 64 and has facilities for swimming, fishing, boating, picnicking, and hiking. A license is required for freshwater fishing, and the Manatee River can also be followed by boat to the Gulf of Mexico. (813) 746-8042.

Madeira Bickel Mound State Archaeological Site is off U.S. 19 about 1 mile south of Terra Ceia and just south of the Sunshine Skyway Bridge. It contains 10 acres of Indian mounds built from 700 to 1400 A.D. by one of the original Indian tribes of Florida, either the Calusas, Aix, or the Tequestas. (813) 722-1017.

Ybor City State Museum is located in the building that once housed the first bakery in Tampa, which provided bread for the entire Latin community. It was built by the Ferlita family and houses fine exhibits of old Tampa and the early cigar-making industry. Surrounding the museum is an outdoor garden that provides a setting for parties, wedding receptions, and other Latin celebrations. Several old homes that were once occupied by cigar-makers and their families have been moved onto lots next to the museum. Included is an exhibit in La Casita, the cigar workers' home. The museum society office and the Ybor Chamber of Commerce offices are also housed there. Operated by the Florida Department of Natural Resources, the museum is located at 1818 9th Avenue in Tampa. This is in an urban area and bicycle riders should be very cautious because of the heavy traffic. Park rangers in the museum will provide information about other historical sites in the area. (813) 247-6323.

Legend

Region 9
South Gulf

Charlotte, Collier, Glades, Hendry, Lee, and
Sarasota counties

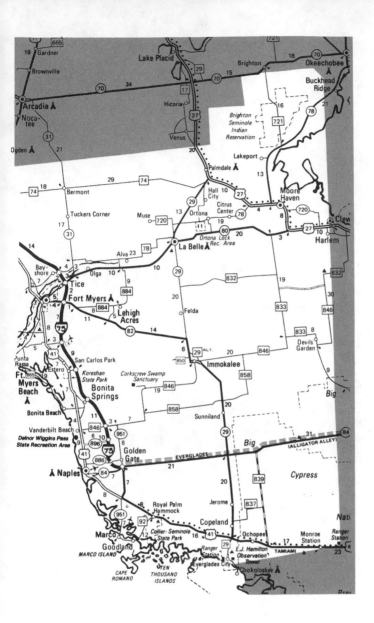

Region 9
South Gulf

◆ This southern stretch of the Gulf Coast is a tropical
dream and the city of Sarasota could be billed as the
cultural center of Florida. It is the home of the oldest
and largest arts council in the state; a half-century-old
community theater; the Sarasota Opera; a symphony;
a concert band; the performing arts hall designed by
associates of Frank Lloyd Wright; and the Ringling
Museums, which include an art museum with paintings
and sculptures by Rubens and other great masters, a
circus museum, and a theater building brought from
Italy—and that's just in Sarasota.

Other cities in this section include Boca Grande, south
of Venice on Gasparilla Island where the Island Bay
National Wildlife Refuge provides a safe home for many
endangered birds. There are a number of estates on this
island with lovely homes. Fort Myers is called the City of
Palms and Thomas Edison spent his winters here for
almost 50 years. His home, laboratory, museum, and
gardens are open for tours. Naples is a wealthy community whose history as a tourist resort dates back to 1887.
One unusual attraction in Naples is a swamp buggy race
track. The races are often featured on ESPN-TV and
provide great fun for competitors and spectators alike.
This entire area is a paradise for bicycle riders.

MUNICIPAL BICYCLE/ PEDESTRIAN COORDINATOR

David Davenport and Greg Wilson, Ft. Myers, (813)
335-2428.

BICYCLE CLUBS

Charlotte County Bicycle Club, P.O. Box 7044, Port Charlotte, FL 33949. Sarasota Bicycle Club, 4318 Rockefeller Ave., Sarasota, FL 33481. Sarasota-Manatee Bicycle Club, P.O. Box 15053, Sarasota, FL 34277; contact Gloria Case (813) 756-8353. Flat Mountain Cycle Club, 110 Tamiami Trail South, Naples, FL 33940.

PLACES OF INTEREST

Collier Seminole State Park features Florida royal palms, a mangrove swamp, cypress swamps, salt marshes, and pine flatwoods. Wildlife include bald eagles, manatees, and black bears. The total park area contains 6,423 acres, of which 4,760 acres are wilderness preserve. A canoe trip can be taken through this area, but permits must be obtained since daily visitors are limited. The park is on U.S. 41 about 17 miles south of Naples and borders the Everglades National Park on the edge of the Gulf of Mexico. There are CAMPING, hiking and picnic areas, some of which are primitive sites. (813) 394-3397.

Delnor-Wiggins Pass State Recreation Area is on a barrier peninsula and covers 166 acres. There is a boat ramp for access to the Gulf of Mexico and a stretch of heavenly beach for swimming, clamming, and shelling. You can reach it by following Gulf Shore Drive out of Naples. (813) 597-6196.

Everglades Reclamation State Historic Site is on U.S. 27 about 10 miles west of Belle Glade. This is where developers first tried to restructure the Everglades for farmland.

Koreshan State Historic Site was built as a religious retreat for members of the Koreshan Unity church who wanted to create a religious utopia in Florida. Judging by the beauty of this site, they nearly succeeded. Located on U.S. 41 where a river empties into the bay at Estero, it contains 305 acres of trails and bridges in a setting of ornamental trees, shrubs, and flowers where tropical birds and wild animals make their home. Visitors can enjoy picnicking, CAMPING, boating, hiking, and a museum. (813) 992-0311.

Myakka River State Park covers 28,875 acres and is one of the largest parks in Florida. It is 17 miles east of Sarasota on State Road 72 and offers visitors a view of what Florida was like before development. Exotic birds and other wildlife make their winter home here and return each fall to breed and raise their young. An area of 7,500 acres is strictly administered, and visitors must register and pay a small fee to enter this area; only 20 people per day are allowed passes and they must follow written instructions in the area. Visitors can also take boat and train tours and enjoy CAMPING, picnicking, fishing, boating, a museum, hiking, cottages, and a snack bar. Boat, canoe, or bicycle rentals are also available. Visitors are warned not to feed the alligators. (813) 924-1027.

Oscar Scherer State Recreation Area is the home of alligators, wild hogs, and Florida scrub jays. It is located on U.S. 41, about 2 miles south of Osprey. The park contains 463 acres and has been left in a natural state, including the primitive CAMPING, picnic, and swimming areas and nature trails. There is a snack bar, and canoes and bicycles can be rented. (813) 966-3154.

A delight for shell-collectors and wildlife enthusiasts are the barrier islands of **Sanibel** and **Captiva,** off the coast near Fort Myers. The islands, connected to the mainland by a toll bridge, can be reached by taking McGregor Boulevard southwest out of Fort Myers. Note that Sanibel Causeway (County Road 867) is closed to bicycles. There are 15 miles of bike paths on Sanibel. Bikers may continue over the small bridge to Captiva, but they will share the road with cars on that island. J. N. Ding Darling National Wildlife Refuge, stretching along the east side of Sanibel, offers a self-guided, 5-mile wildlife drive; canoe trails and rentals; foot trails; and a nature center. Visitors may see alligators, ospreys, wading birds and other wildlife, particularly during the winter months.

Wiggins Pass State Recreation Area is on State Road 401 off U.S. 41, about 6 miles south of Bonita Springs. Visitors can enjoy picnics, swimming, fishing, or boating in this park.

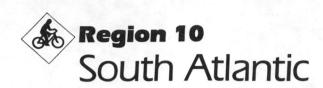

Region 10
South Atlantic

Indian River, Martin, Palm Beach, and
St. Lucie counties

Legend

HIGHWAY TYPES — PRIMARY — TOLL HIGHWAYS — SECONDARY — CONNECTING — NEARING COMPLETION — UNDER CONSTRUCTION — ROUTE NUMBERS

CONTROLLED ACCESS

Multi Lane Divided	Ⓗ Rest Area with Rest Rooms
	▲ Rest Area without Rest Rooms

79 279 U.S. Interstate

| 2 & 3 Lane Undivided | Interchange |

1 191 U.S. Federal

Capital ★ County Seat ◉ ✈ Passenger Service Airport

OTHER HIGHWAY CLASSIFICATIONS

| Paved Divided | Distances in MILES between diamonds and outlined cities |

1 19 191 State and Provincial

10 8

| Paved Undivided | City |

AAA Designated Scenic Byway

Campground in Area (Check CampBook)

Town

| Gravel | Customs Stations |

G11 County and Local

Auto & Passenger
Ferries
Passenger Only

| Earth | |

153

Region 10
South Atlantic

◆One of the fastest-growing metropolitan areas in the United States is Florida's south Atlantic Coast. It has been difficult for regional planners to maintain open access to this area's beaches as skyscraper condominiums and resort hotels crowd the ocean's edge. Florida Atlantic University was built in the early 1960s on a 1200-acre campus at the outer edges of Boca Raton, but the growth of the city now surrounds the campus.

Vero Beach is the shipping center for the famous Indian River citrus. Jupiter is the home of a Florida State University theater built and donated by Burt Reynolds. It is used for training aspiring performing artists and playwrights. Reynolds also spends time at his ranch in Jupiter when he is working on films at Disney Studios.

Palm Beach is home to some of the wealthiest and most exclusive people in Florida. The winter season in Palm Beach features polo matches attended by Prince Phillip of England, sports car racing, dog races, and jai alai. Henry Morrison Flagler, the man who founded Palm Beach, built Whitehall for a summer home there in 1901 at a cost of $4 million. It is now a museum open to the public.

On the southeastern tip of Lake Okeechobee is the city of Belle Glade, where truck-farming produces 32 varieties of vegetables. The Port of Belle Glade on the Okeechobee Waterway provides barges, yachts, and cruisers with cross-state access to the Atlantic Ocean and the Gulf of Mexico. The months of January and February are crowded with water events including the Belle Glade, Lake Okeechobee, and Clewiston fishing tournaments. There is plenty to see and do in this region, but you should contact local bicycle clubs for best times and places to travel by bicycle.

MUNICIPAL BICYCLE/ PEDESTRIAN COORDINATOR

Ronnie Blackshear, West Palm Beach, (407) 684-4170

BICYCLE CLUBS

Pahokee Wheelmen, c/o Rev. A. F. Donovan, 870 E. Main St., Pahokee, FL 33476. Wheelers of Kings Point, Bertha Soloman, 673 Saxony, Delray Beach, FL 33446. West Palm Beach Bicycle Club, P.O. Box 6581, West Palm Beach, FL 33405; contact Michael McGee at (407) 736-7858.

PLACES OF INTEREST

Fort Pierce Inlet-St. Lucie Museum State Recreation Area is located in part on Jack Island and Pepper Beach. A museum along the ocean offers exhibits and a mural depicting the history of the area and treasures salvaged from shipwrecks. Parking is located on State Road A1A and visitors must cross a footbridge to get to the park, where no cars are allowed. There is picnicking, swimming, hiking, a snack bar, and an observation tower for viewing the 119 species of birds that have been sighted here. (305) 468-3985.

Jonathan Dickinson State Park is near the site where a group of Quakers, traveling from Jamaica to Philadelphia, were shipwrecked in 1696. They were captured by Indians but managed to talk their captors into

guiding them north through the Florida jungles to St. Augustine. Naturalist Jonathan Dickinson was the leader of this group and he wrote in his journals about their adventure. The journals were later published and are considered today to be one of the finest records of unsettled Florida. Mangrove swamps, scrub pine flatlands, and exotic plant life still abound in this 10,284-acre park. Bald eagles, manatees, and Florida sandhill cranes live within this park. It is located on U.S. 1, about 3 miles north of Jupiter, and visitors can enjoy CAMPING, picnics, swimming, fishing, boating, cottages, a snack shop, and horseback tours. There are boats, canoes, and bicycles for rent. (305) 546-2771.

Jupiter Inlet Lighthouse was built in 1860 and is one of the oldest lighthouses along the Atlantic Coast. The museum contains artifacts from old shipwrecks and is open free on Sundays.

Loxahatchee National Wildlife Refuge is about 13 miles northwest of Delray Beach on U.S. 441. It is a wetland area covering nearly 150,000 acres and is home to Everglades kites, cranes, herons, and alligators. Two recreation areas—Twenty-Mile Bend to the north and Loxahatchee to the south—are open during daylight hours except on holidays.

Pahokee State Recreation Area is in the middle of the city of Pahokee, on the Hoover Dike at Lake Okeechobee. There is a 30-acre site for CAMPING, fishing, swimming, boating and picnicking. (305) 436-1626.

Sebastian Inlet State Recreation Area is on a barrier island on State Road A1A and is the site of the McLarty Museum. This is where survivors of a Spanish treasure fleet found refuge in 1715 when their ships were sunk in a hurricane. Most of the treasure was not salvaged until the 1950s, and replicas of the coins and artifacts are on exhibit in the museum, along with a diorama and other displays. There is CAMPING, picnicking, swimming, fishing, boating, and a snack shop. (305) 727-1752.

Region 11
South Florida and the Keys

Broward, Dade, and Monroe counties

Legend

HIGHWAY TYPES	PRIMARY	TOLL HIGHWAYS	SECONDARY	CONNECTING	NEARING COMPLETION	UNDER CONSTRUCTION	**ROUTE NUMBERS**

CONTROLLED ACCESS

| Multi Lane Divided | | U.S. Interstate |
| 2 & 3 Lane Undivided | | U.S. Federal |

Rest Area with Rest Rooms
Rest Area without Rest Rooms

Interchange
Capital County Seat Passenger Service Airport

OTHER HIGHWAY CLASSIFICATIONS

Paved Divided	Distances in MILES between diamonds and outlined cities	State and Provincial
Paved Undivided	City Campground in Area (Check CampBook)	AAA Designated Scenic Byway
Gravel	Town Customs Stations	Auto & Passenger Ferries Passenger Only	County and Local
Earth		

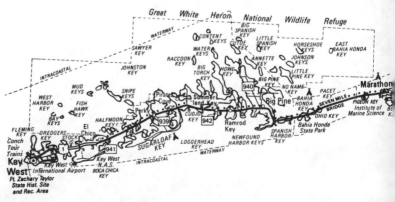

160

Deerfield Beach
Hillsboro Beach
Lighthouse Point
Pompano Beach
Lauderdale-by-the-Sea
Coral Springs
Tamarac
Plan-
tation
Fort Lauderdale
Hugh Taylor Birch
State Park
Lloyd Beach
State Recreation Area
Hollywood
Hallandale
Golden Beach
Bal Harbour
Miami Beach
Surfside
Opa-
Locka
Hialeah
Miami Springs
Miami Beach
MIAMI
VIRGINIA KEY
KEY BISCAYNE
Sweet-
water
Barnacle
State Historic Site
S. Miami
Coral
Gables
Key Biscayne
Bill Baggs
Cape Florida
St. Rec. Area
Ken-
dall
Perrine
Howard
SOLDIER
KEY
Goulds
Princeton
Homestead
Air Force
Base
RAGGED KEYS
SANDS KEY
Biscayne
National
Park
ELLIOTT
KEY
Homestead
Park
Hdqrs. &
Visitor
Center
Florida
City
OLD
RHODES
KEY
John Pennekamp
Coral Reef
State Park
KEY
LARGO
To Key West
Key Largo

Big
Garden
Devil's
Garden
Cypress
Big
Seminole
Big
Cypress
PARKWAY
(ALLIGATOR ALLEY)
Indian
Reservation
National
Preserve
Everglades
National
Ochopee
Monroe
Station
Ranger
Station
TAMIAMI
Paolita
Ranger
Station
Indian
Village
Indian
Village
TRAIL
TRAM TOUR
Chekika
State
Recreation
Area
Observation
Tower
Lostmans River
Patrol Station
SHARK POINT
Pa-hay-okee
Overlook
Pineland
Trail
Ranger
Station
Park
Royal Palm
Interpretive
Center
Mahogany
Hammock
Paurotis
Pond
Nine Mile
Pond
West
Lake Trail
Mangrove Trail
CAPE
SABLE
NORTHWEST
CAPE
CAPE SOUND ROAD

Everglades National Park
To Florida City
To Homestead & Miami-Miami Beach
Barnes
Sound
Terrapin Bay
Little
Trout
Cove
Snipe
Point
EAGLE
KEY
DEER
KEY
BOGGY
KEY
NEST
KEYS
CHRISTIAN
POINT
FLAMINGO RANGER
STATION VISITOR
CENTER & MARINA
SHARK
POINT
MOSQUITO
POINT
PASS
KEY
LAKE
KEY
John
Pennekamp
Coral
Reef St. Pk.
Key Largo
OYSTER
KEY
PALM
KEY
RANKIN
KEY
BIG
MADEIRA
POINT
BLACK
BETSY KEYS
SHELL
KEY
Bay
Newport
Rock Harbor
FRANK
KEY
ROSCOE
KEY
BUTTON
WOOD
KEYS
RUSSEL
KEY
MANATEE
KEY
BUTTERNUT
KEYS
RODRIGUEZ
KEY
Thompson
CLUETT
KEY
CORINNE
KEY
CALUSA
KEYS
STAKE
KEY
SPY
KEY
BOB ALLEN
KEYS
PANHANDLE
KEY
CRAB
KEYS
WEST
KEY
CRANE
KEYS
Tavernier
TAVERNIER KEY
BARNES
KEY
COTTON KEY
WINDLEY KEY
PLANTATION
KEY
Plantation
Islamorada
SHELL
KEY
Theater of the Sea
UPPER
MATECUMBE
KEY
KEYS
LIGNUMVITAE
KEY
HIGHWAY
LOWER
MATECUMBE
KEY
FLORIDA
WATERWAY
FIESTA
KEY
Long Key
State Park
Layton
LONG KEY
INTRACOASTAL
BURNT
POINT
CONCH
KEY
OVERSEAS
LONG KEY
VIADUCT
Duck Key
Marathon
Airport
GRASSY
KEY
KEY
VACA
Key Colony
Beach
931

161

Region 11
South Florida and the Keys

This last region of Florida is every bit as wonderful to visit as are the other parts of the state. It includes the exciting city of Miami, the truck farms of Homestead where much of our winter vegetables are grown, the Everglades National Park, and the spectacular Florida Keys. The southern tip of Florida curves out into the Gulf of Mexico and trails to an end only 90 miles from the coast of Cuba in a string of islands. Henry Flagler first connected the 112 miles of islands with narrow highways and 42 bridges as part of the Flagler railroad. At the end of this string of islands is the city of Key West.

Key West is a popular spot among artists and writers and is the year-round home of singer Jimmy Buffett. Ernest Hemingway lived here and his home is now open to visitors. The city is known by local residents as "The Conch Republic" after they attempted to secede from the United States. U.S. 1 out of Homestead has been improved with new roadways and bridges, and there is space designated for walkers or bikers on both sides of U.S. 1 most of the way to Key West.

Public campgrounds are well located all down through the Keys, and there are also a number of private campgrounds including a very unique one in Old Key West. Jabours Trailer Park does not boast about its lush tropical setting or its planned activities. It's just a gravel-covered parking lot, but location is everything and this campground is in Old Town Key West within walking distance of all the great spots. The folks who run it will even furnish free padding to soften the gravel under your tent.

From this campground you can walk over to the docks
for a half-day of fishing in the Gulf or the ocean on a
charter boat for only $15. When you get back to the
docks they'll clean and fillet your fish for you. In the
afternoon you can explore Mel Fisher's Treasure
Museum, take a ride on the Conch Train, cook your
fresh fish over the campfire, and then watch a spectacular sunset on the beach.

There are some highways in this region that are not
suitable for bicycling, such as U.S. 41 east of Miami. It is
very narrow and dangerous, even for cars, so be very
careful and avoid riding on this road.

MUNICIPAL BICYCLE/ PEDESTRIAN COORDINATOR

Mark Horowitz, Ft. Lauderdale, (305) 357-6661; Jeff
Hunter, Miami, (305) 375-4507.

BICYCLE CLUBS

Several bicycle clubs are scattered through this region
and they all welcome visitors. The Everglades Bicycle
Club, P.O. Box 430282, South Miami, FL 33243. Coral
Way Bicycle Club, 2241 Coral Way, Miami, FL 33145.
Bicycle Club of Homestead, P.O. Box 1155, Homestead,
FL 33030. Coconut Grove Bicycle Club, Box 696, Coco-
nut Grove, FL 33145. Bicycle Generation, c/o Lee
Cordery, 807 SE 8th St., Deerfield Beach, FL 33441. BC
Wheelers, 600 NW 183 St., Miami, FL 33169. Bike Tech
Cycling Club, 14230 SW 62 St., Miami, FL 33183; (305)
382-9291. Broward Wheelman Bicycle Club, P.O. Box
7242, Ft. Lauderdale, FL 33338; contact Larry Tibbs

(305) 968-8211. South Broward Wheelers, P.O. Box 5022,
Hollywood, FL 33083; contact Barry Steinberg (305)
987-7387. Key Biscayne Bicycle Club, 260 Crandon Blvd.
#6, Key Biscayne, FL 33149.

STATE BICYCLE TRAILS

Route J: The Gold Coast—30 miles of flat terrain
through the southern suburbs of Miami (see page 73).

Route K: The Everglades—170-mile tour of the tip of
Florida (see pages 73–74).

PLACES OF INTEREST

Bahia Honda State Recreation Area is on the
Atlantic Ocean and offers 276 acres of beach-front facilities including CAMPING, picnicking, swimming, fishing,
diving, boating, and gift and snack shops. It's located 7
miles south of Marathon at the Seven Mile Bridge. Visitors should contact the park office for reservations. (305)
872-2353.

Barnacle State Historic Site is along Biscayne Bay
on Main Highway in Coconut Grove and features the
restored home of Ralph Munroe, who was a pioneer set-
tler in the area.

Bill Baggs Cape Florida State Recreation Area
is on the southern tip of Key Biscayne, just south of the
town of Key Biscayne. The Key lies southeast of Miami.
The park features the historic Cape Florida Lighthouse
in a 406-acre setting. There are guided tours, picnicking,
fishing, swimming, boating, diving, and a snack bar.
(305) 361-5811.

Bill Baggs
CAPE FLORIDA
STATE RECREATION AREA

Chekika State Recreation Area is north of Homestead at 237th Street and Grossman Drive, west of State Road 27. The park's 640 acres surround artesian springs which pump out about 3 million gallons of fresh water daily. Visitors can enjoy CAMPING, swimming, picnics, fishing, and hiking. (305) 253-0950.

Hugh Taylor Birch State Recreation Area is in Fort Lauderdale on State Road A1A and offers 180 acres of Atlantic beach-front swimming, boating, diving, and picnicking facilities. (305) 564-4521.

John Pennekamp Coral Reef State Park at Key Largo draws visitors from throughout the world. Its unique features include almost 55,000 acres of underwater coral reef. It was the first underwater state park in the United States. If visitors plan ahead they can enjoy CAMPING, fishing, picnics, swimming, snorkeling, diving, boating and hiking. Visitors can also rent boats, canoes, and bicycles and buy souvenirs in the gift shop. It is very important to make reservations at this park because it is usually full year-round. (305) 451-1202.

Lignumvitae Key State Botanical Site is accessible only by boat and contains a restored mansion located on an island off the coast at Islamorada. (305) 664-4815.

Long Key State Recreation Area is about 15 miles south of Islamorada on U.S. 1. It contains facilities for CAMPING, picnic areas, fishing, boating, swimming, diving, and hiking. (305) 664-4815.

Lloyd Beach State Recreation Area covers 243 acres between Dania and Fort Lauderdale and features picnicking, swimming, fishing, diving, and boating. There is no park ranger station here but the park is open from sunrise to sunset.

Everglades National Park can be reached on the southern end by following U.S. 1 to Florida City and then taking State Road 27 south to Flamingo. From the northern end take U.S. 41 south from Naples and turn right on County Road 29 to the park station at Everglades City. The subtropical wilderness of this park is unique in all the world. There is CAMPING and wilderness canoe trips down through the heart of the swamp where nights are spent on sleeping platforms supported by poles sunk in the waters of the channels.

The U.S. Park Service rangers delight in sharing the stories of their special world with visitors and will supply maps of the trails or brochures about the wildlife. They also conduct leisurely walking tours of their domain, pointing out the snowy egrets, wood storks, roseate spoonbills and the American bald eagles that nest in the park in the winter months. The 300,000-acre park contains most of the remaining wild crocodiles in the United States. The park is open all year and bicycle tourists are most welcome.

The Seminole Indian Reservation of Hollywood covers about 400 acres. It is one of five Seminole Reservations in Florida. The tribal headquarters are at the intersection of U.S. 441 and Stirling Road in Hollywood. The Seminoles also maintain reservations at Brighton, Big Cypress, Immokalee, and Tampa. The annual Tribal Fair and Rodeo is held at the Hollywood Reservation in early February and features arts and crafts, alligator wrestling, and the Seminole Indian Stomp Dancers, as well as American Indian dancers from reservations across the United States. Like other snowbirds, these dancers are happy to come down from Montana and North or South Dakota for a little winter warmth as part of the Indian National Cultural Exchange program. (305) 321-1000.

The Miccosukee Indian State Reservation is headquartered in Homestead and contains 333.3 acres. Located along U.S. 41, known to the native people as "The Trail," it stretches for 5.5 miles and is only 500 feet wide. The Tribe has a restaurant and an Indian village which are open to the public. Their annual Fair and Festival is held the last week of the year and features dancers from across the country. Colorful patchwork clothing, authentic beaded jewelry, and hand-carved cypress canoes are exhibited and sold. Visitors can get a unique view of the Everglades Swamp by taking a ride on one of the Miccosukee Indian airboats. (305) 223-8380.

Appendix—Useful Addresses

State Government

FLORIDA STATE BICYCLE DIRECTOR
Dan Burden, Director of Bicycle Programs or
Pat Pieratte, Assistant
Florida Department of Transportation
Haydon Burns Bldg.
605 Suwannee St.
Tallahassee, FL 32304
(904) 488-4640

DEPARTMENT OF NATURAL RESOURCES
Division of Recreation and Parks
Marjory Stoneman Douglas Building
3900 Commonwealth Blvd.
Tallahassee, FL 32399

STATE TOURISM OFFICE
Division of Tourism
107 W. Gaines St.
Tallahassee, FL 32301

FISHING AND HUNTING LICENSES
Division of Law Enforcement
Department of Natural Resources
3900 Commonwealth Blvd.
Tallahassee, FL 32304

STATE AND COUNTY ROAD MAPS
($0.30 a sheet or $25.00 for full set—minimum order $1.00)

FLORIDA BICYCLE TRAILS MAPS
(Seven different sets of maps and local information covering
one- to six-day trips—$1.00 each set)
Florida Department of Transportation
Maps and Publications Sales
Mail Station 12
605 Suwanee St.
Tallahassee, FL 32301-8064

RECREATION AND CAMPING MAPS/
BIANNUAL EVENTS CALENDAR
Bureau of Education & Information
Department of Natural Resources
3900 Commonwealth Blvd.
Tallahassee, FL 32304
(904) 488-7326

U.S. Government
NATIONAL PARKS IN FLORIDA:
United States Forest Service
227 Bronough Street
Tallahassee, FL 32301
(904) 681-7266

FLORIDA ORGANIZATIONS
Florida Bicycle Association
P.O. Box 16652
Tampa, FL 33687
1-800-FOR-BIKE

Florida Council of American Youth Hostels, Inc.
P.O. Box 1108
Tallahassee, Florida 32302
(904) 878-2042

The Florida Trail Association, Inc.
P.O. Box 13708
Gainesville, FL 32604

League of American Wheelmen in Florida
Jim and Mary Fortney
Rt. 6, Box 609
North Loop Road
Pensacola, FL 32507
(904) 492-0046

Effective Cycling in Florida
John Bates, Instructor
5604 Antoinette St.
Sarasota, FL 34232
(813) 371-6104

OUTSIDE FLORIDA

Rails-to-Trails Conservancy
1400 16th St. NW
Washington, DC 20036
(202) 797-5400

Bikecentennial
P.O. Box 8308
Missoula, MT 59807

League of American Wheelmen
Suite 209, 6707 Whitestone Road
Baltimore, MD 21207

Sierra Club
530 Bush Street
San Francisco, CA 94108

Bicycle Federation of America
1818 R Street NW
Washington, DC 20009

International Human-Powered Vehicle Association
Box 51255
Indianapolis, IN 46251

OTHER PUBLICATIONS
Florida Bicyclist
3491-11 Thomasville Road, Suite 115
Tallahassee, FL 32308
(904) 562-9086

Florida Bicycle Trails
Order Form

See pages 70–74 for descriptions of these state-designated trails.

Currently, maps of routes A,B, D, E, F, G, and H are available for purchase at a cost of $1.00 each.* Maps of routes C, I, J, and K are not available yet.

Please indicate which maps you have enclosed payment for:

___ Route A: Sugar Beaches
___ Route B: Canopy Roads
___ Route D: Crystal Springs
___ Route E: The Healing Waters Trail
___ Route F: Lakes-'n-Hills
___ Route G: Withlacoochee Meander
___ Route H: Land O'Lakes

(   ) Please let me know when maps of routes C, I, J, and K may be purchased.

_____

NAME (PLEASE PRINT)

_____

ADDRESS

_____

CITY   STATE   ZIP CODE

Total Amount Enclosed $ _____

Order From: Florida Department of Transportation
            Map and Publication Sales, MS 12
            605 Suwannee Street
            Tallahassee, FL   32301

Make check or money order payable to Florida Department of Transportation. Do not send cash.

*All orders shipped to Florida addresses must include 6% state sales tax.

**Florida Dept. of
Transportation
Map and Publication Sales**
Mail Station 12
605 Suwannee Street
Tallahassee, FL 32301

Phone (904) 488-9220

General Highway County Maps
½" = 1 mile 18" × 27"
$.30 per sheet (Some counties have
more than one sheet)

_____ ALACHUA
_____ BAKER
_____ BAY
_____ BRADFORD
_____ BREVARD (2 sheets)
_____ BROWARD
_____ CALHOUN
_____ CHARLOTTE
_____ CITRUS
_____ CLAY
_____ COLLIER (2 sheets)
_____ COLUMBIA (2 sheets)
_____ DADE (2 sheets)
_____ DESOTO
_____ DIXIE
_____ DUVAL
_____ DUVAL INSET
_____ ESCAMBIA
_____ FLAGLER
_____ FRANKLIN
_____ GADSDEN
_____ GILCHRIST
_____ GLADES
_____ GULF
_____ HAMILTON
_____ HARDEE
_____ HENDRY (2 sheets)
_____ HERNANDO
_____ HIGHLANDS (2 sheets)
_____ HILLSBOROUGH (2 sheets)
_____ HOLMES
_____ INDIAN RIVER
_____ JACKSON
_____ JEFFERSON
_____ LAFAYETTE

_____ LAKE (2 sheets)
_____ LEE
_____ LEON
_____ LEVY (2 sheets)
_____ LIBERTY
_____ MADISON
_____ MANATEE
_____ MARION (2 sheets)
_____ MARTIN
_____ MONROE (3 sheets)
_____ MONROE INSET (2 sheets)
_____ NASSAU
_____ OKALOOSA
_____ CKEECHOBEE
_____ ORANGE
_____ OSCEOLA (2 sheets)
_____ PALM BEACH (2 sheets)
_____ PASCO
_____ PINELLAS
_____ POLK (2 sheets)
_____ PUTNAM
_____ ST. JOHNS
_____ ST. LUCIE
_____ SANTA ROSA
_____ SARASOTA
_____ SEMINOLE
_____ SUMTER
_____ SUWANNEE
_____ TAYLOR
_____ UNION
_____ VOLUSIA (2 sheets)
_____ WAKULLA
_____ WALTON
_____ WASHINGTON

Minimum order is $1.00 plus tax. Payment must be included with order.
All orders being sent to a Florida address must include 6% sales tax. Please
furnish a street address and telephone number for shipping by UPS. Make
check or money order payable to Florida Department of Transportation.
Do not send cash.

Blue-line copies may be substituted if our supply of printed maps
is exhausted.

Complete set (UNBOUND) of General Highway County Maps is $25.00 plus
6% sales tax.

Please help us improve this book.

A book like *The Florida Bicycle Book* is never finished.
As hard as we have tried to make this book as complete
and enjoyable as possible, we know that those out biking
in Florida will find new information that should be in
this book. We would very much appreciate your sending
us that information so that we might consider adding
it to the next edition. Please send any comments or
information to

> Jackalene Crow Hiendlmayr
> c/o Pineapple Press
> P.O. Drawer 16008
> Southside Station
> Sarasota, FL 34239

We will carefully evaluate your comments.

Thanks and happy biking.